LGBTQI+ IN THE BASQUE COUNTRY

Basque Politics Series No. 17

LGBTQI+ IN THE BASQUE COUNTRY

MARTA LUXAN, JONE MIREN HERNANDEZ,
AND XABIER IRUJO

CENTER FOR BASQUE STUDIES
UNIVERSITY OF NEVADA, RENO
2020

This book was published with generous financial support from the Basque Government.

Center for Basque Studies
University of Nevada, Reno
1664 North Virginia St,
Reno, Nevada 89557 usa
http://basque.unr.edu

Cover Design by Derek Thornton

LIBRARY OF CONGRESS CATALOGING-IN-PUBLICATION DATA

Names: Luxán Serrano, Marta, editor. | Miren Hernandez, Jone, editor. |
  Irujo Ametzaga, Xabier, editor.
Title: LGBTQI+ in the Basque Country / edited by Marta Luxán Serrano, Jone
  Miren Hernandez, Xabier Irujo Ametzaga.
Description: Reno, Nevada : Center for Basque Studies Press, 2020. |
  Series: Conference papers series ; no. 18 | Includes bibliographical
  references.
Identifiers: LCCN 2020031623 | ISBN 9781949805253 (paperback)
Subjects: LCSH: Sexual minorities--Spain--Pais Vasco--History. | Gender
  identity--Spain--Pais Vasco--History. | Homosexuality--Spain--Pais
  Vasco--History. | Sexual minorities--France--Pays Basque--History. |
  Gender identity--France--Pays Basque--History. |
  Homosexuality--France--Pays Basque--History.
Classification: LCC HQ73.3.S66 P35 2020 | DDC 305.30946/6--dc23
LC record available at https://lccn.loc.gov/2020031623

tents

Prologue

In the fall of 2018, Xabier Irujo, director of the Center for Basque Studies at the University of Nevada, Reno, proposed publishing a compilation of LGBTQI+-related research conducted in, or about, the Basque Country. This idea launched the adventure upon which the Center and the Master's in Feminist and Gender Studies of the Universidad del País Vasco/Euskal Herriko Unibertsitatea (UPV/EHU) would embark, leading us to a variety of harbors.

The idea was to create a common place where researchers from multiple disciplines and varied approaches could shed light on LGBTQI+ issues in the Basque context. We were also particularly interested in building bridges between the LGBTQI+ movement and the academic world, and in publishing a compilation of articles that reflect the situation in the Basque Country. This book is one of the fruits of our collaboration. Its main goal is to encourage both more study and action, as well as to highlight the need to generate written references related to LGBTQI+ topics.

This collection does not represent all of the research conducted in the Basque study of LGBTQI+ issues, nor all of the people working on them, whether through activism or academics. It is, rather, a snapshot, including different perspectives, markedly from university researchers, but also those with obvious connections to activism. It is, therefore, an invitation to continue to discuss, rethink, and write more about LGBTQI+ issues from diverse shores, harbors, and seas.

In this collection's eight chapters, legislative issues, the mission of social movements and of their subjectivities, and a historical perspective on lesbianism and homosexuality are covered. Additionally, an attempt to understand bodies beyond binary categories is made, and an examination of cultural expressions is presented through literary analysis.

In the first chapter, Irujo offers a historical and international view of the rights of the LGBTQI+ community from the eighteenth century to the present day. Among other issues, the author highlights the fact that the World Health Organization declassified homosexuality as a disease in 1990, just thirty years ago. He also outlines the historical development of legislation relating to sexual freedoms and the recognition of civil rights to same-sex couples in both Europe and the United States.

Next, Andrea Bartomeu sheds light on legislation as it relates to sexual orientation and gender identity in the Autonomous Community of the Basque Country. In addition to a comprehensive review of the regional (autonomous) regulations, the author presents a critical assessment of the scope and adequacy of the current regulations. Bartomeu highlights the need to bring legislation into line with a complex and kaleidoscopic reality that faces specific challenges. She proposes incorporation of international recommendations to ensure both that transsexuality is not treated as pathological and the effective protection of the rights of transgender people. In this regard, one of the crucial issues presented is the right to self-determination of one's own gender. Finally, despite its brevity, her discussion on LGBTQI+ asylum seekers is particularly relevant.

María Ruiz Torrado guides us into social movements, particularly those of feminist groups. From an anthropological perspective, Ruiz analyzes the impact of queer discourses and practices on feminist communities in the Basque Country since the beginning of the twenty-first century. The chapter includes three thematic points: the origins and development of the queer movement and theory in the West; the incidence and characteristics of queer discourse in Basque feminist groups; and the uniqueness of the practice of queer activism in the Basque Country.

Regarding queer discourse, the central idea is to understand that both gender and sex are social constructs that can (and should) be deconstructed. As for queer practice, the focus is on both political activism in relation to the individual militants' experiences and on the effort to combine protest with entertainment. The author describes a space inhabited by small, interconnected, multiregional activist groups that have a flexible understanding of militancy and that incorporate tools such as performances, BDSM practices, and Drag King workshops.

In the next article, Jokin Azpiazu Carballo proposes a metaphor—fast, slow, and still waters—for analyzing the main debates and entanglements developing around LGBTQI+ policies in the Southern Basque Country.

This sociologist describes a changing landscape, based on both individual and group interviews, in which processes converge at different speeds.

Azpiazu refers to the development of "pink capitalism," the normalization of identities, and the impact of neoliberal policies on LGBTQI+ people, as *fast waters*. As a response to the fast movement of those developments, the subjects of this research have developed openly anticapitalist positions. As such, the author focuses the discussion on the subjects' personal experience and the role that their experiences play in redefining the political landscape and in the construction of identities, in an area of *slow waters* that, nevertheless, is in constant negotiation with the previous. Finally, Azpiazu argues that we are in a moment in which strategies used by the movement would have been exhausted, in which political positions and alliances would be redefined. Despite this moment being one of *still waters*, it poses a potentially transformative challenge, the author says.

Using both autobiographical and scientific approaches, María Gómez looks at the ways of understanding intersexuality, as well as a genealogy of the concept itself. Through her own bodily journey, Gómez analyzes the relationship between her own body and activism, distinguishing three stages that she calls *encounters and confusion; deconstruction and agency;* and *me, intersex.*

Relying on the idea that sex, gender, and sexuality are sociocultural constructs, the author advocates for an end to the binary sexual model and the construction of new inclusive categories. In addition, she argues that the only way to do this is to create networks among different disciplines, as well as between health-care workers and intersex people, friends, and families. Finally, she presents an emotional call to defend the rights of intersex people.

Maialen Aranguren and Abel Díaz, Experiencia Moderna Research Group (UPV/EHU) (Modern Experience), contribute the historical insight to this collection through an account of part of their work within the project titled "The Experience of Modern Society in Spain: Emotions, Gender Relations, and Subjectivities."

Aranguren provides a historical reading on the evolution of the political subject of the feminist movement and the debates surrounding it. In particular, she analyzes the discursive framework of the Basque Feminist Movement and Emakumearen Sexual Askatasunerako Mugimendua (ESAM) and lesbian collectives between 1977 and 1994, paying special attention to the political significance given to the identities of *woman* and *lesbian.* In other words, she describes the evolution of the political subject of the feminist movement and the impact that lesbianism had on the process.

The action begins in 1977, with the celebration of the first Basque Women's Days/Basque Women's Conference. The author reviews different positions within feminism to account for the debate around sexuality, lesbianism, and its potential as a destructive element of patriarchy. In addition, she pauses in 1979, when the first group of Basque lesbians, ESAM, was formed, and discusses the evolution of its political discourse.

For his part, Abel Díaz goes back to the first Franco regime to analyze both the transformation of the way in which homosexuality was understood and the place it occupied in the social construct of the dictatorship, such as the social and criminal sanctions associated with these behaviors.

Through the analysis of court documents, the author describes the period immediately after the war of 1936 as a time when the reprobation of homosexuality was closely linked to Catholic morals and, therefore, the relationship between crime and sin is presented as inseparable. Later, in the 1950s, medical discourses became increasingly more important, and justice focused on the repression of deviant bodies, the repressive mechanisms of those discourses becoming more intense through an amendment made in 1954 to the Law of "Vagos y Maleantes" (Vagrancy Act) of 1933.

As a conclusion to this collection, literary critic Ibon Egaña Etxeberria reflects on what is meant by LGBTQI+ literature and analyzes how non-heteronormative lives have been represented in Basque literature. He underlines the importance of the cultural context, as well as the power relationships and the symbols of domination present in cultural representations of minorities.

Egaña structures his analytical proposal around four themes: the nation and the construction of a national discourse that acts as a totalizing umbrella of other conflicts and tensions; stories that travel between different territories, in which homosexual identity and national identity intertwine; what the author refers to as *lesbian reinventions*; and, more recently, stories about precarious lives and imperfect happiness. Finally, the author offers some provocative reflections that, rather than concluding the text and/or the book, suggest the need to continue working on these issues.

Enjoy!

Hernani, February 2020

Marta Luxán Serrano

Head of the Master's of Feminist and Gender Studies

1

The Struggle for LGBTQI+ Rights at the International Level

Xabier Irujo

University of Nevada, Reno, Center for Basque Studies

Hague, July 7 [1730]. The Baron Van Renswoude, First Noble of the Province of Utrecht, does not yet appear, but is said to be gone to Venice. Be that as it will, he has been formally divested of all his Employs, and was charged home by several of the Wretches executed both at the Hague and at Utrecht, who gave him the horrid Appellation of Bougre Bougrissimo [Greatest of all Buggers]. This is the more extraordinary, because he is on the wrong Side of 70. At Amsterdam there has been a sort of Decimation introduced; Four of those detested Criminals have been publickly executed there, Two of them were half strangled, then burnt with Straw; and the other Two cast into large Tons [tuns, barrels], and drown'd upon a Stage. After this, they were all Four carry'd and thrown into the Zuyder Zee, where 30 others were drown'd in Sacks a few Days before, with Cannon Bullets at their Feet. The second Citations against some that disappear, were expected the 3d or 4th Instant, but were postponed, as it is presumed, till the State has made a more severe Law against that abominable Vice.[1]

Homosexuality has historically been considered an aberration by most religions and a *crimen nefandum* (atrocious crime), classified as a crime of sodomy in most countries of the world. The ruins of the nave of the Saint Martín Cathedral of Utrecht (known as *Domkerk*) had become a meeting place for homosexuals in the city until, in April 1730, the authorities began an investigation at the request of the sacristan, Josua Wils. Two soldiers were arrested and interrogated, and by virtue of their confessions,

Zacharias Wilsma, who stated that there were homosexual networks and meeting places in other parts of the Dutch Republic, was arrested. This initiated a wave of proceedings. The authorities issued an edict comparing the situation in the Netherlands with that of Sodom and Gomorrah, which in the opinion of the edict's authors had also been punished by God for their sins *against nature*.[2] The edict contained six articles in which it was specified that sodomy had never before been treated as a criminal offense, but which henceforth it was to be prosecuted with the full weight of the law and the prisoners publicly executed. According to the sacred scriptures, the penalty for sodomy should be death; it was up to the judge to determine the manner of execution, which should be exemplary and commensurate with such an execrable crime. Anyone who collaborated in favoring, sustaining, or concealing networks of homosexual relationships would also be condemned to death. The bodies of the executed were to be immediately incinerated and their remains thrown into the sea, without Christian burial. The proceedings and the names of the accused and those who had escaped were to be made public. Finally, the absences of public officials between May and August 1730 were to be investigated to ascertain whether they were persons who tried to escape from justice for reasons of sodomy.[3]

In Utrecht alone, some forty people were tried, all men, of whom eighteen were sentenced to death and strangled. Death by strangulation in private was the most common punishment for homosexual acts in the Dutch Republic, but other punishments during the purge of 1730 and 1731 included hanging and drowning in barrels of water. Following the ordinance, the remains of those convicted were burned and thrown into the sea. About 250 men were called to testify before the authorities: sixty were sentenced to death, and ninety-one were sentenced in absentia to the penalty of banishment.[4] The trials continued between 1730 and 1737, with new outbreaks of violence in 1764 and 1776. Following the occupation of the Netherlands and the constitution of the Batavian Republic (*Bataafse Republiek*) in 1795, the number of sodomy prosecutions rose again until 1803. By the end of the eighteenth century, about 600 people had been prosecuted for sodomy in the Netherlands. It was not an exception, although the causes and the charges varied from one country to another. In Sweden, for example, 600–700, mostly adolescent boys, were sentenced to death on charges of zoophilia, but there were hardly any charges of sodomy.[5]

In Catholic countries, the levels of repression were similar. Lieutenant General Jean Charles-Pierre Lenoir, of the Paris police, for example, conducted a census of 20,000 sodomites in the city. Jean Diot and Bruno Lenoir were the last homosexuals accused of sodomy to be executed in France. Both were publicly burned at the stake at Place de Grève in Paris on July 6, 1750, together with the documents of the judicial process. Their ashes were scattered and their property confiscated by the crown. As recorded by their lawyer, who witnessed the execution: "The fire was composed of seven wagons, 200 faggots [bundles of wood sticks] and straw. They were attached to two stakes and strangled beforehand, and were they immediately burned with shirts impregnated with sulphur. They did not publicly cry the sentence, apparently to avoid mentioning the name and nature of the crime."[6] Thirty-three years later, Commissioner Michel Foucault made a new calculation of 40,000 sodomites in the capital of the Republic.[7]

With the onset of the French Revolution, the situation began to change. Although the sexual rights of the individual are not mentioned in the Declaration of the Rights of Man and of the Citizen of August 1789, the French Penal Code of 1791 did not include the crime of sodomy or any other mention of sexual relations between persons of the same sex. This policy of decriminalization of the practice of homosexuality remained in the Penal Code of 1810, as well as in the countries and colonies dominated by the French empire that adopted these codes between 1791 and 1812. Among the first countries to decriminalize sodomy between 1792 and 1795 are the French Republic, Andorra, Haiti, Monaco, Luxembourg, and Belgium.

Although nothing was regulated in these first codes, in 1832 the French State set the age of consent for sexual activity at eleven years for both sexes, which in 1863 would be increased to thirteen years. There was no mention of the relations between individuals of the same sex, which were still considered immoral, and the practice of which was pursued under a plethora of laws relating to morality and public order in most European countries. Thus, the July 19-22, 1791, law on decency, for example, passed months before the above-mentioned penal code, included in the eighth article of the second title that, "Those accused of having committed a gross public indecency, by a public offense against the decency of women, by unseemly actions, by displaying or selling obscene images, of having encouraged debauchery, or having corrupted young people of either sex, will be immediately arrested."[8] Articles 330 and 334 of the Penal Code of 1810 echoed these same measures that did not clearly distinguish between homosexual relationships and pederasty, by prescribing that any person accused of indecency or corruption of youth could be sentenced to up to two years of imprisonment and imposed a fine of 50 to 500 francs.

Sodomy was a crime in all North American colonies before 1776. Some states imposed the death penalty, while others such as Georgia replaced it with life imprisonment, but in many states the punishments continued to be draconian. For example, the revision of the Virginia Penal Law proposed by Thomas Jefferson established that anyone found guilty of rape, polygamy, or sodomy with man or woman would be punished; if he was a man, he would be castrated, and if she was a woman the cartilage of her nose would be perforated, producing a hole at least half an inch in diameter.[9]

In 1811, after decades of persecution, the Netherlands, now liberated from French rule, adopted the Penal Code of 1791 which, as we have seen, did not contemplate sodomy in its articles. This didn't introduce any positive regulation of sexual relations nor did it allow sexual activity between two adult persons of the same sex in private. Although the last execution for sodomy in the kingdom of France was in 1750, having sexual relations with a person of the same sex under the age of twenty-one was considered sodomy until 1982 in the French Republic.

Notwithstanding all this, the Code of 1791 and the Dutch case opened a chain of processes of decriminalization throughout the entire world which, after 200 years, remains open. In 1887, Giuseppe Zanardelli, Italy's minister of justice, removed the references to the stigmatization of homosexuals in the new penal code that was adopted throughout the territory of the Kingdom of Italy and the Vatican in 1889 and took effect a year later. Zanardelli's strategy was to leave the "unnamed vices" (*vizi innominabili*) out of the code by removing the crime of sodomy from the penal code and establishing the age of consent for sexual acts to fourteen years, regardless of gender.[10] This obviously did not prevent police or social repression, and the Zanardelli Code was revoked in 1930 by Mussolini, who introduced the Rocco Code, which prohibited and punished homosexuality under Article 528 with prison terms of six months to three years for public scandal.[11] A directive prohibiting discrimination on the basis of sexual orientation in Italy would not be adopted until 2003, and civil unions between people of the same sex would not be adopted until 2016.

A number that is not exhaustive, more than 100 countries and some territories have decriminalized homosexual relations between 1811 and 2019. This does not mean the practice was not persecuted or regulated. In fact, one must wait until the end of the nineteenth century to observe the first regulations on sexual relations between people of the same gender.

One of the earliest examples of regulation of same-sex relations is Poland, where, in 1948, the established age of consent for all sexual acts, homosexual or heterosexual, was fifteeen years. Although immigration laws banned homosexuals from entering the United States from 1952 to 1990, the LGBTQI+ movement gained strength from the uprising of Stonewall Inn in New York on June 28, 1969. One of the first laws on gay rights in the US was in East Lansing, Michigan, in March 1972. Also in the spring of 1972, San Francisco became one of the first US cities to pass an ordinance banning discrimination on grounds of sexual orientation by any city official.[12] Malta legalized homosexuality in 1973. as did Croatia, Montenegro, Slovenia, and the province of Vojvodina in 1977. The Homosexual Law Reform Act was passed in New Zealand in 1986, which amended the Crimes Act by decriminalizing and regulating sexual relations between men over the age of sixteen, who until then could be sentenced to up to five years in prison for "homosexual indecency."[13] In Liechtenstein, Section 129 of the Penal Code of 1852 was repealed in 1989, decriminalizing male homosexuality and establishing the age of consent at eighteen years, when the age for heterosexual and lesbian couples was sixteen.[14]

One of the countries that stands out with regard to LGBTQI+ legislation is Sweden. Sexual activity between people of the same sex was decriminalized in 1944 and the age of consent of eighteen was established in 1972, although it would not equate to that of heterosexual couples (age fifteen) until 1978. Also in 1972, transvestism was declassified as a disease, making Sweden the first country in the world to allow transsexuals to legally change their sex, providing free hormone therapy through public health care. Following this model, Chile passed a similar law in 1974, allowing transsexuals to legally change their name and gender in the civil registry. In 1979, several people in Sweden declared themselves sick for being homosexuals, in protest of the classification of homosexuality as a disease. A group of activists occupied the headquarters of the National Board of Health and Welfare and shortly afterward Sweden became the first country in the world to remove homosexuality from the list of illnesses.[15] The World Health Organization declassified homosexuality as a disease in 1990 and the American Medical Association in 1994.

Starting in 1987, Sweden became the first country to pass laws protecting the LGBTQI+ community in relation to social services, taxes, and inheritance[16] and one of the first to legislate against discrimination based on sexual orientation. The Swedish penal code was amended in 1987 to include a law banning discrimination on the basis of sexual orientation.[17] Following this model, the Canadian province of Nova Scotia passed a law against discrimination on the grounds of sexual orientation in 1991; one year later, the same law was adopted in New Brunswick, and British Columbia; and in 1995, in Newfoundland and Labrador. A year later Canada's parliament approved the measure at the federal level. The New Zealand parliament would also approve in 1993 an amendment to the human rights law, banning discrimination on the grounds of sexual orientation or of being affected by human immunodeficiency virus. Other countries followed this example (South Africa in 1994, Bulgaria and the United Kingdom in 2003, Portugal in 2004 . . .) finally opening the doors to legalization of same-sex marriage.

The Danish parliament was the first to enact, in 1989, the laws of registered partnership (similar to a civil union) for same-sex couples, with most of the same rights as marriage (excluding the right to adoption until June 2010 and the right to marriage in a church).[18] The laws of civil union and registered partnership were approved and went into effect in Norway in 1993.[19] Sweden followed the model in 1995, Greenland in 1996, and Iceland in 1996.[20] In all cases, the laws on homosexual couples did not take into consideration all the rights of a heterosexual marriage, such as the right to adoption.

Not until the twenty-first century were the first rules approved on the adoption of Swedish-born and non-Swedish-born children by registered same-sex couples in Sweden (on February 1, 2003),[21] and since 2005 lesbian couples have had the same access to in vitro fertilization and assisted insemination that heterosexual couples have. On April 2, 2009, the *Washington Post* reported that the Swedish parliament had passed a law granting same-sex couples the same rights as heterosexual couples.[22] Sweden became the first country in the world to legalize same-sex marriage, and the law went into effect May 1, 2009. In 2013, legislation allowing for the legal change of gender without hormone replacement therapy and sex reassignment surgery was adopted. Until the beginning of 2017, the Swedish National Board of Health and Welfare automatically applied the diagnosis of "gender dysphoria" to transgender patients. But following the World Health Organization's decision to eliminate transsexualism from the chapter on mental illness in its diagnostic guide, the Swedish parliament approved its declassification as a mental illness just two years ago.[23] The United Nations health agency announced in 2018, in the eleventh revision of the International Classification of Diseases (ICD), that the term "gender incongruence" refers to people whose gender identity is different from that of their birth gender and has been removed from the organization's chapters on mental disorders and sexual health. The change was presented to the World Health Assembly, the WHO's legislative body, in 2019, and will take effect on January 1, 2022, three years later.[24]

In the United States, California passed the first laws on civil union and registered partnership in 1999 and recognized the right of adoption in 2001. That same year, the Netherlands passed the law on same-sex marriage contemplating the right of adoption. These examples laid the model that would later be applied in practically all the states of western Europe and countries of the Commonwealth.[25]

The last laws on sodomy were overturned by the US Supreme Court in the case *Lawrence v. Texas* in 2003. The Supreme Court of Massachusetts in the same year ruled in *Goodridge v. Department of Public Health* that the state's constitution did not allow the banning of same-sex marriage, thereby opening the gap that would allow, twelve years later, same-sex marriage throughout the country. However, this tide of policies for the equalization of rights for heterosexual and homosexual marriages also generated a strong counterreaction in 2004, the third year of the first presidential term of George W. Bush. The states of Mississippi, Missouri, Montana, Oregon, and Utah banned gay marriage, and the states of Arkansas, Georgia, Kentucky, Louisiana, Michigan, North Dakota, Ohio, Oklahoma, and Wisconsin banned both marriage and civil unions between same-sex couples. In 2004, forty US states had laws against marriage or same-sex unions.[26]

In the face of this wave of prohibitions, San Francisco City Hall, with Mayor Gavin Newsom at the helm, began issuing marriage licenses to same-sex couples in February 2004. Newsom declared that the equal protection clause of California's constitution gave him the authority to grant marriage licenses to people of the same sex.[27] Dorothy L. T. Del Martin and Phyllis Ann Lyon, a lesbian couple known to be gay rights activists who had been living together for 54 years, were the first couple to marry in the San Francisco City Council on Thursday, February 12, opening the doors to six months of express weddings. I was there. In anticipation that the courts would immediately revoke the issuance of marriage licenses, a human tide arrived from all parts of the country. A long line of couples waiting for their marriage license circled several times around City Hall. The building overflowed with the influx of people, and, coincidentally, the meeting of the Basque Government delegation, of which I was part, headed by the minister of justice, Joseba Azkarraga, with Newsom had to be delayed. There weren't enough witnesses for all the couples, so we acted as witnesses for some of them. In just the first ten days of express weddings, more than 3,000 same-sex couples applied for and obtained their marriage licenses.[28] It would be given the name "The Winter of Love."

On Friday, February 13, the Proposition 22 Legal Defense and Education Fund, and the Campaign for California Families, filed a case in the San Francisco Superior Court requesting the city be immediately banned from granting marriage licenses to same-sex couples.[29] On Wednesday, February 18, 2004, President Bush said that the city of San Francisco was issuing licenses against the law and that he would support the law to protect marriage between a man and a woman. Two days later, California governor Arnold Schwarzenegger instructed Bill Lockyer, the state attorney general, to prosecute the measures taken by Newsom, and he said he was confident the law would be enforced by the courts. And, indeed, even given Lockyer's reluctance, who personally favored equal rights for homosexual and heterosexual couples, on August 12, 2004, the state supreme court unanimously ruled that the city and county of San Francisco had exceeded their authority and violated state law by issuing marriage licenses to same-sex couples. The court also declared invalid all 8,072 same-sex marriages performed in San Francisco based on licenses obtained from February to August 2004.[30]

In the United States, civil marriage is governed by state law; however, Congress in 1996 passed the Defense of Marriage Act (DOMA), whose Section 3 defined marriage as "a legal union between one man and one woman as husband and wife, and the word 'spouse' refers only to a person of the opposite sex who is a husband or a wife."[31] In 2005, while a number of western European and Commonwealth countries passed laws on same-sex marriage, the White House-driven policy of banning same-sex marriage and civil unions penetrated the states of Alabama, South Carolina,

Colorado, South Dakota, Idaho, Kansas, Tennessee, Texas, Virginia, and Wisconsin. Nevertheless, in May 2008, the California Supreme Court awarded same-sex couples in that state the right to marry, and Martin and Lyon were remarried, once again becoming the first same-sex couple to be wed. However, California's Marriage Protection Act, known as Proposition 8, which took effect on November 5, 2008, once again banned same-sex marriage, and the same thing happened in Arizona and Florida.[32] Despite this, marriages that occurred between the decision of the Supreme Court of California and the approval of Proposition 8 were considered valid.

Eventually, things began to change with Barack Obama's entry into the White House in 2009. Obama became, in May 2012, the first US president to publicly announce his support for same-sex marriage. The US Supreme Court, in *United States v. Windsor*, ruled that Section 3 of the Defense of Marriage Act was unconstitutional for violating the Fifth Amendment of the US Constitution, and thus granted federal recognition of same-sex marriage on June 26, 2013.[33] Between 2012 and 2014, same-sex marriage laws were adopted and went into effect in a number of states and in several reservations. The US Supreme Court in June 2015 ruled in *Obergefell v. Hodges* that it was a fundamental right of same-sex couples to marry in the same terms and conditions as opposite-sex couples, under the Fourteenth Amendment of the Constitution.[34] As a result, since 2015, same-sex marriage has been legal in all fifty states. In addition to this, Mississippi's ban on adoption by same-sex couples on March 31, 2016, was dismissed and on June 26, 2017, in *Marisa N. Pavan, et al. v. Nathaniel Smith*, the US Supreme Court overturned a ruling of the Arkansas Supreme Court and ordered all states to treat same-sex couples the same as opposite-sex couples, thus reaffirming the right of adoption by same-sex couples in all fifty states.[35] As we can see, within the European framework, the greatest advances have been made from legislation, and progress in the United States has occurred primarily in the courts of justice.

In the European Union (EU), on September 12, 1989, the European Parliament passed a resolution on discrimination against transsexuals and the inclusion of gender identity as grounds for asylum. Through this non-binding resolution, Parliament considered that transsexuality was a psychological and medical problem, but also the problem of a society incapable of accepting a change in the culturally established roles of the sexes, and that human dignity and personal rights must include the right to live in accordance with one's sexual identity. Parliament considered: The surgical procedure for transsexuals to change their sex was not yet available or not regulated in all member states of the Union. The costs in question were not reimbursed by public health institutions. Transgender people were still discriminated against, marginalized, and sometimes even criminalized, with an unemployment rate of between 60 percent and 80 percent among transsexuals undergoing a sex change. So Parliament called on member states to enact provisions on the right of transsexuals to change sex through endocrinology, plastic surgery, and aesthetic treatment, and to ban discrimination against them. Parliament also asked that in addition to regulating medical and psychological treatment, the states would adopt legal measures for the protection and legal recognition of name changes and sex changes on birth certificates and identity documents.[36] Finally it called on the Council of Europe to enact a convention for the protection of transsexuals, which has yet, in 2019, to see the light of day.

A second step in the work of the European Parliament for the rights of the LGBTQI+ community was the adoption of the Roth Report on February 8, 1994. Through this declaration, Parliament affirmed its conviction that all citizens should be treated equally. The fundamental principle of equal treatment should be applied, irrespective of the sexual orientation of each individual, in all the legal provisions already adopted or that could be adopted in the future. Parliament also considered that the Treaties of the European Communities should establish firmer provisions for the protection of human rights. It therefore called on the Community institutions to make preparations, in the context of the institutional reform scheduled for 1996, to establish a European institution capable of guaranteeing equal treatment. Likewise, Parliament called on the European Commission and the European Council to adhere to the European Convention on Human Rights, provided for in the 1990 Community program, as a first step toward a more vigorous protection of human rights.[37]

Parliament reminded member states to eliminate all legal provisions that criminalize and discriminate against same-sex sexual activities, to establish the same age of consent for homosexual and heterosexual activities, and to end the unequal treatment of persons with homosexual orientation through legal and administrative provisions. Discriminatory measures were typical of many European states—for example, the United

Kingdom had discriminatory provisions in place to curb the alleged "spread of homosexuality." Parliament, however, called on all states to take measures and initiate campaigns against the increasing number of acts of violence against homosexuals and to ensure the prosecution of perpetrators of these acts of violence. Finally, it recommended that member states take measures to ensure that social and cultural organizations of gay women and men have the same access to public funds as other social and cultural organizations.[38]

Parliament called on the Commission of the European Communities to present a draft recommendation on equal rights for homosexual men and women and to submit a report to Parliament, at five-year intervals, about the situation of gay men and women in Europe. The report's writers felt that such a recommendation should, at a minimum, try to end the different and discriminatory ages of consent for homosexual and heterosexual acts; the prosecution of homosexuality as a public nuisance or indecency; all forms of discrimination in labor and public law; discrimination in criminal, civil, contractual, and commercial law; the electronic storage of data relating to the sexual orientation of a person without their knowledge or consent and the unauthorized disclosure or misuse of such data; and the prohibition of gay couples from marriage or a legal equivalent. The recommendation also strived to guarantee the full rights and benefits of marriage, allow the registration of partnerships, and remove any restriction of the rights of lesbians and homosexual men to be parents or to adopt or raise children.[39]

Although it was not a binding report, some European countries, from 1994 onward, pushed for new measures for the rights of the LGBTQI+ community. Since then, the European Parliament has continued to work at three different levels: amending commission legislation to reflect the rights of LGBTQI+ people; drawing up reports or resolutions which, although not legally binding, can become important tools in the political context of the EU and influence the member states' legislative processes via monitoring and interpellating the work of the Council and the European Commission; and organizing public hearings in the European Parliament to raise awareness and encourage debate. Parliament's efforts, without legislation, however, mean that the greatest progress in safeguarding the rights of the LGBTQI+ community has been through the jurisprudence of the European courts, rather than through Parliament or other European institutions.

A significant demonstration in the process of recognition of LGBTQI+ rights in Europe was the inclusion, in the 1997 Treaty of Amsterdam, of article 19 (ex article 13), which empowered the European Union to "take appropriate action to combat discrimination based on sex, racial or ethnic origin, religion or belief, disability, age or sexual orientation."[40] The adoption of this measure led to the adoption of the Employment Directive of 2000, which obliged all member states to introduce legislation prohibiting discrimination in employment on several grounds, including sexual orientation, by December 2003. The directive therefore obliged countries wishing to join the EU to introduce said legislation. Given the number of countries affected, the Employment Directive is arguably the most important single legislative initiative in the history of LGBTQI+ rights in Europe. The Community Action Programme to Combat Discrimination, with an expenditure of 100 million euros from 2001 to 2006, was also launched to combat discrimination in several areas, including sexual orientation. The revision of the 1976 Equal Treatment Directive in 2002 also meant that discrimination based on gender identity, i.e., discrimination related to the identity of a transgender person or the process of gender reassignment, would infringe upon the Employment Directive of the year 2000. The deadline for implementation in member states was set for October 2005.

In 2000, the EU also adopted the Charter of Fundamental Rights of the European Union, including the prohibition of sexual orientation discrimination in its Article 21, becoming the first international human rights charter to do so. The charter became compulsory after the Treaty of Lisbon took effect on December 1, 2009. These developments made it possible that sexual activity between people of the same sex was legal in all EU states in 2019, and employment discrimination on grounds of sexual orientation has been banned since 2000. However, EU states have different laws regarding the protection of LGBTQI+ rights within civil unions or marriage between same-sex couples and adoption rights of these couples.

As far as the United Nations is concerned, it did not deal with the rights of the LGBTQI+ community until September 1995. That year, in preparation for the Fourth World Conference on Women, sexual orientation was debated in the negotiations on the draft of the Beijing Declaration. In the autumn of 1994, the International Gay and Lesbian Human Rights Commission (IGLHRC) organized a petition urging governments to "recognize the right to determine one's sexual identity; the right to control one's body, particularly in establishing intimate relationships; and the right to choose if, when, and with whom to bear or raise children, as fundamental components of the human rights of all women regardless of sexual orientation."[41] On the penultimate day of the conference, Beverley Palesa Ditsie, the South African representative of the Lesbian Caucus, addressed the entire assembly on the importance of guaranteeing the rights of the lesbian community. During this debate, the Holy See, some Catholic countries, and a good number of Islamic countries showed a strong opposition to the mention of sexual orientation. Some of the delegates, such as those from Sudan and Yemen, made especially virulent statements against homosexuality.[42] Although the proposal on the inclusion of the expression "sexual orientation" in Paragraph 96 of the draft was finally rejected, it was the first time that there were discussions on this topic within the UN and the first time that member states had taken an explicit position, although limited, about the recognition of homosexuality within the framework of the rights of women.[43]

In April 2003, Brazil caught activists and other governments by surprise by proposing, in the Commission on Human Rights in Geneva, a resolution entitled "Human rights and sexual orientation," inspired by the Universal Declaration of Human Rights. The Holy See joined Pakistan in opposing the text, arguing that it could be understood as a tolerance toward pedophilia. In addition, it was reported that the Holy See called the capitals of some Latin American member states to ensure abstentions or a vote against the resolution. Finally, consideration of the resolution was postponed until the Commission on Human Rights of 2004.[44] However, it would not be until 2006 that Norway submitted a joint statement on human rights violations based on sexual orientation and gender identity, on behalf of fifty-four member states, in the Commission on Human Rights. In said document these states commended the attention paid to these issues by various public and private institutions and called on everyone to continue to integrate the consideration of human rights violations related to individuals' sexual orientation and gender identity.[45]

In 2008, led by Argentina, sixty-six member states supported a declaration, within the UN General Assembly, confirming that international protection of human rights includes sexual orientation and gender identity. The statement had an unprecedented amount of support, including states across five continents, and reaffirmed the principle of non-discrimination, which requires that human rights be applied equally to all human beings, regardless of their sexual orientation or gender identity. The declaration condemned killings; torture; arbitrary arrest; deprivation of economic, social, and cultural rights (including the right to health); violence; harassment; discrimination; exclusion; stigmatization; and prejudice directed against individuals in all countries of the world by virtue of sexual orientation or gender identity.[46] This statement drew a backlash from the Arab League and the Organization of Islamic Cooperation in opposition to LGBTQI+ rights. Both statements remain open for ratification, neither of them having been officially adopted by the General Assembly to this day.

It would not be until 2010 that the UN began to take positive steps in the defense of LGBTQI+ rights. On December 10, 2010, the International Day of Human Rights, the secretary-general delivered the first of several speeches on the decriminalization of homosexuality and other measures to combat violence and discrimination based on sexual orientation and gender identity. Wherever there is tension between cultural attitudes and universal human rights, rights must prevail, he said. According to his data, homosexuality was still considered a crime in seventy countries. Among the major legal obligations of member states in the protection of human rights of LGBTQI+ people is to protect individuals from homophobic violence by repealing laws that criminalize homosexuality, he said.[47]

The reaction took no time. The General Assembly on July 17, 2011, requested that the United Nations high commissioner for human rights establish a study to be completed by December 2011. The study would document discriminatory laws and practices and acts of violence committed against persons because of their sexual orientation and gender identity in all regions of the world. The study would also consider the manner in which international human rights law can be applied to end the violence and related human rights violations motivated by sexual orientation and gender identity. The request also included the organization of a roundtable during the nineteenth session of the Human Rights Council, based on the data of the study established by the high commissioner, to conduct a constructive, informed, and transparent dialogue about discriminatory laws and practices and acts of violence committed against persons because of their sexual orientation and gender identity. This request was approved with twenty-three votes in favor, nineteen against, and three abstentions.[48] It was the first resolution of this kind and was hailed as historic.

The report, published in December 2011, enumerated violent acts against LGBTQI+ people, including the murder of 680 people in fifty countries from 2008 to 2011. Seventy-six countries preserved criminal laws related to sexual orientation or gender identity. According to those who drafted the report, such laws, including the so-called "sodomy laws," were often relics of legislation from the colonial era. In at least five countries, the death penalty still applied to those found guilty of offenses related to consensual homosexual behavior between adults. Accordingly, the report established as obligations of member states under international human rights law: to protect the right to life, liberty, and safety of individuals, regardless of their sexual orientation or gender identity; to prevent torture and other cruel, inhuman, or degrading treatment on the grounds of sexual orientation or gender identity; to protect the right to privacy and against arbitrary detention on the grounds of sexual orientation or gender identity; to protect individuals from discrimination on the grounds of sexual orientation and gender identity; and, to protect the right to freedom of expression, association, and assembly in a nondiscriminatory manner.[49]

The high commissioner for human rights, Navi Pillay, recommended that member states should: (a) Promptly investigate all reported killings and other serious incidents of violence perpetrated against persons because of their actual or perceived sexual orientation or gender identity, whether in public or in private, whether by the state or not; (b) Take measures to prevent torture and other forms of cruel, inhuman, or degrading treatment on the grounds of sexual orientation and gender identity, investigating all reported incidents of torture and ill treatment for the firm purpose of prosecuting and holding accountable those responsible; (c) Ensure that no one who escapes persecution on the grounds of sexual orientation or gender identity is returned to a territory where their life or freedom is threatened, and that asylum laws and policies recognize that persecution as owing to their sexual orientation or gender; (d) Repeal laws used to criminalize individuals on grounds of their homosexuality (for engaging in consensual sexual conduct with members of the same sex) and equalize the age of consent for heterosexual and homosexual conduct; ensure that other criminal laws are not used to harass or detain people for their sexuality or gender identity and expression; and abolish the death penalty for offenses related to consensual sex; (e) Enact comprehensive antidiscrimination legislation that includes, among prohibited practices, discrimination based on sexual orientation and gender identity, and recognizes forms of discrimination that intersect; guarantee that the fight against discrimination on the basis of sexual orientation and gender identity is included in the mandates of national human rights institutions; (f) Ensure that individuals are able to exercise their rights to freedom of expression, association, and peaceful assembly in safety, without discrimination on the basis of sexual orientation and gender identity; (g) Implement adequate awareness and training programs for police, prison officers, border guards, immigration officers, and other law enforcement officials, and support public information campaigns to combat homophobia and transphobia among the general public, as well as campaigns directed against homophobia in schools; (h) Facilitate legal recognition of transgender persons' preferred gender and establish agreements to allow relevant identity documents to be reissued to reflect the gender and preferred name, without infringing on other human rights.[50]

In 2013, the United Nations conducted its first ministerial meeting on the rights of the LGBTQI+ community. Pillay, the United Nations high commissioner for human rights, said that after the publication of the 2011 report, numerous member states had begun to implement legislative reforms to prohibit discrimination on grounds of sexual orientation, combat violent actions against LGBTQI+ people and raise public awareness. In September 2014, Brazil, Chile, Colombia, and Uruguay led a follow-up resolution at the United Nations Commission on Human Rights. In a second resolution on human rights, sexual orientation, and gender identity (A/HRC/RES/27/32), the United Nations high commissioner for human rights was again asked to update the 2011 report A/HRC/19/41 to share best practices and ways to overcome violence and discrimination, in accordance with the existing rules and international human rights laws, and to submit it to the twenty-ninth session of the Commission. The petition was approved by a vote of twenty-five to fourteen. It was the first time in the Comission's history that a resolution on LGBTQI+ rights was adopted by the majority of its members, which was interpreted as a trend toward greater support by member states to address these problems at the international level.[51] The update was presented to the Human Rights Council in June 2015.

An important step forward was finally taken in 2016 when a resolution was adopted on June 30, requesting that the independent expert of the United Nations Human Rights Council submit an annual report to the council beginning at its thirty-fifth session in 2017, and to the General Assembly at its seventy-second session in 2017-18. The resolution's authors

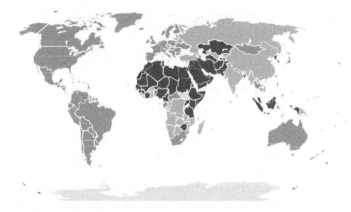

STATES THAT SIGNED the LGBTQI+ rights declaration in the General Assembly or in the Human Rights Council in 2008 or 2011 (in dark gray) and states that supported the opposition statement in 2008 and 2011 (in black). Unfortunately, religious arguments among groups have influenced the debate on LGBTQI+ rights.

also urged member states to cooperate with the independent expert to implement the expert's mandate, including by providing all the information requested, seriously considering requests to visit their countries, and applying the recommendations in the expert's reports. Finally, the writers encouraged everyone to cooperate fully with the independent expert and requested that the secretary-general and the United Nations high commissioner for human rights provide the independent expert with all necessary human, technical, and financial resources required for the effective fulfillment of the mandate.[52] Also in 2016, the UN Security Council condemned the mass shooting at the Orlando, Florida, nightclub Pulse, the first time in history that this council acknowledged violence directed at the LGBTQI+ community.

This long-term mandate of an independent expert is probably the most manifest expression in support of the LGBTQI+ community's rights at the UN to this day. In 2018, twenty-five more countries recognized same-sex marriage. Nevertheless, as of April 2019, same-sex marriage is banned in seven EU member states (Bulgaria, Croatia, Hungary, Latvia, Lithuania, Poland, and Slovakia). Only thirteen of the twenty-eight member states respect the seven basic pillars of LGBTQI+ rights: recognition of same-sex couples; right to marriage; right to adoption; right to adoption in couples; criminal laws for crimes based on sexual orientation; laws against discrimination in all areas; and the right to serve in the army.[53] Generally, the countries of Eastern Europe, which have been recently integrated into the Union, are the ones with the greatest deficits in this area. At the international level, as of April 2019, ten countries, all of them predominantly Islamic, impose the death penalty for homosexuality: Afghanistan, Brunei, Iran, Mauritania, Pakistan, Qatar, Saudi Arabia, Sudan, Yemen, and the United Arab Emirates. The same laws also govern some constituencies in Iraq, Nigeria, Syria, and Somalia.

The resolutions of 2011, 2014, and 2016 are an important step forward in the normalization and protection of the rights of LGBTQI+ people internationally. But it is obviously quite insufficient. The legal coverage of the rights of this social sector at the international level continues to be lacking today. There are many reasons and immense gaps. Fundamentally, the documents cited are mere resolutions or statements of intentions limited to making recommendations to the member states. But no agreement in effect positively binds the signatory countries. While there are references to individual freedom regarding sexual orientation, positive instruments regarding gender identity are rare. So, for example, the Charter of Fundamental Rights of the European Union, in Article 21, states that any discrimination of an individual is prohibited, and in particular that by reason of gender or sexual orientation, but the declaration does not mention the right to freely express one's own gender identity.[54]

Certainly, we are still far from living in a civilized world, if by civilized we mean a world in which the basic rights of humanity are fully respected. There is no binding convention on this subject in the European Union. We must not underestimate, in any case, the progress that has been made in the last forty years of activism in the fight for the comprehensive recognition of human rights. Nor should the work of all the people who have been involved in this process for decades be undervalued. Debate about the nature of LGBTQI+ rights that some countries have put in place is widespread. To cite one example, in Europe, a larger number of young people are renouncing marriage as an institution, whether religious or civil. Consequently, some LGBTQI+ groups criticize that marriage between people of the same gender is considered an "achievement." What in the 1970s, '80s, or '90s was a challenge for the LGBTQI+ community, today is either no longer a challenge or has become an even bigger one. But that must not lead us to deny the progress that has been made in LGBTQI+ rights from 1969 to the present day.

While there has been much progress at the legal level, there is still a lot to be done politically, socially, and culturally. Although a greater number of countries are adopting laws on nondiscrimination on the basis of sexual orientation, societies are still not as receptive to this spectrum of rights as might be desired. However, achievements at the legal level are necessarily based on a prior social awareness. The adoption and implementation of laws on the protection of human rights also influence the people's cultural traditions. In short, there is still a long way to go and much work to do with regard to the full legal undertaking and socialization of the rights of the LGBTQI+ collective in particular, and of human rights in general. Necessary steps are being taken in this direction, but these achievements almost always come too late and too slowly. They are always accompanied by rejection by a large sector of society. Perhaps the day will come when most of the world's population is ashamed of the fact that, throughout history, small collectives have had to fight to convince the whole of humanity of the need to protect freedom and equality and to guarantee the full respect of all human rights—political, economic, social, and cultural. That day has yet to arrive.

BIBLIOGRAPHY

Boele-Woelki, Katharina and Angelika Fuchs, eds. *Legal Recognition of Same-sex Couples in Europe*, Antwerp & New York: Intersentia, 2003.

Cahill, Sean. *Same-sex Marriage in the United States: Focus on the Facts,* Lanham, MD: Lexington Books, 2004.

Corrêa, Sonia, Rosalind Petchesky and Richard Parker. *Sexuality, Health and Human Rights*, London & New York: Routledge, 2008.

Crew, Louie and Ellen M. Barrett. *The Gay Academic*, Palm Springs, CA: ETC Publications, 1978.

Crompton, Louis. *Homosexuality and Civilization*, Cambridge, MA: Harvard University Press, 2006.

Den Otter, Ronald C. *In Defense of Plural Marriage*, Cambridge, MA: Cambridge University Press, 2018.

Faderman, Lillian. *The Gay Revolution: The Story of the Struggle*, New York: Simon & Schuster Paperbacks, 2016.

Fone, Byrne, *Homophobia: A History*, New York: Henry Holt and Company, 2013.

Gerstner, David A., *Routledge International Encyclopedia of Queer Culture*, Hoboken, N: Taylor and Francis, 2012.

Girard, Françoise, "Negotiating Sexual Rights and Sexual Orientation at the UN", in E. Parker, R. Petchesky, and R. Sembler, eds. *SexPolitics: Report from the Front Lines*, Rio de Janeiro: Sexuality Policy Watch, 2007.

Markowitz, Fran and Michael Ashkenazi, eds. *Sex, Sexuality, and the Anthropologist*, Urbana, IL: University of Illinois Press, 1999.

Mezey, Nancy J. *LGBT Families*, Los Angeles: SAGE, 2015.

Norton, Rictor. *Mother Clap's Molly House: The Gay Subculture in England*, 1700–1830, East Haven, CT: GMP, 1992.

O'Halloran, Kerry. *The Politics of Adoption: International Perspectives on Law, Policy & Practice*, New York: Springer, 2015.

O'Keeffe, David and Patrick M. Twomey. *Legal Issues of the Amsterdam Treaty*, Oxford: Hart Publishing, 1999.

Parker, Richard, Rosalind Petchesky, and Robert Sember, eds. *SexPolitics: Reports from the Front Lines*, Rio de Janeiro: Sexuality Policy Watch, 2007.

Pinello, Daniel R. *America's Struggle for Same-Sex Marriage*, Cambridge, MA: Cambridge University Press, 2006.

Pires Marques, Tiago. *Crime and the Fascist State, 1850-1940*, New York: Routledge, 2016.

Porterfield, Jason. *Marriage Equality: Obergefell v. Hodges*, New York: Enslow Publishing, 2017.

Ragan, Bryant T. *Homosexuality in Modern France*, Oxford: Oxford University Press, 1996.

Smith, Kevin B. *State and Local Government*, Washington, DC: CQ Press, 2005.

Simon, Rita J. and Alison Brooks. *Gay and Lesbian Communities the World Over*, Lanham, MD: Lexington Books, 2009.

Tin, Louis-George. *Diccionario Akal de homophobia*, Tres Cantos: Akal, 2015.

West, Thomas G. *The Political Theory of the American Founding: Natural Rights, Public Policy, and the Moral Conditions of Freedom*, Cambridge, MA: Cambridge University Press, 2017.

Wintemute, Robert and Mads Andenæs, eds, *Legal Recognition of Same-sex Partnerships: A Study of National, European and International Law*, Oxford: Hart Publishing, 2001.

NOTES

 1 *London Journal*, London, July 4, 1730. http://rictornorton.co.uk/eighteen/1730news.htm
 2 Fone. *Homophobia: A History.*
 3 Crew. *The Gay Academic*, 86-87.
 4 Norton. *Mother Clap's Molly House: The Gay Subculture in England*, 253.
 5 Fone. *Homophobia: A History.*
 6 Crompton. *Homosexuality and Civilization*, 450.
 7 Tin. *Diccionario Akal de homophobia*, 378.
 8 Ragan. *Homosexuality in Modern France*, 82-82.
 9 West. *The Political Theory of the American Founding*, 231.
 10 Pires. *Crime and the Fascist State*, 97.
 11 Mussolini's decree did not affect the Vatican which was an independent state, so the Zanardelli Code is still in effect .
 12 *California Journal*, vol. 6, 1975, p. 343.
 13 *The New Zealand Law Reports*, vol. 2, 2003, p. 822.
 14 Gerstner. *Routledge International Encyclopedia of Queer Culture*, 660.
 15 Markowitz. *Sex, Sexuality, and the Anthropologist*, 122.
 16 Law 232 of May 14, 1987, and Law 813 of June 18, 1987, on the property of homosexual

or heterosexual domestic partners. Law 1117 of June 23, 1994, establishing that registered civil cohabitation would have the same effect as marital unions, with the exception of the right of adoption, custody of minors, and artificial insemination. See, *Yearbook of Private International Law*, vol. 5, 2004, p. 193.

17 Simon. *Gay and Lesbian Communities the World Over*, 89.

18 Boele-Woelki. *Legal Recognition of Same-sex Couples in Europe*, 13.

19 Wintemute. *Legal Recognition of Same-sex Partnerships: A Study of National, European and International Law*, 438.

20 Boele-Woelki. *Legal Recognition of Same-sex Couples in Europe*, 10.

21 O'Halloran. *The Politics of Adoption: International Perspectives on Law, Policy & Practice*, 332.

22 Simon. *Gay and Lesbian Communities the World Over*, 89.

23 "Swedish government orders study into mental health conditions of transgender people," *The Local: Swedish News in English*, www.thelocal.se, 2017.

24 Pickman, Ben and Brandon Griggs. "The World Health Organization will stop classifying transgender people as mentally ill," CNN, http://edition.cnn.com, June 20, 2018.

25 Also in 2001, laws on civil or registered union (without the right of adoption until October 2004) were adopted in Germany, in Finland (civil or registered union law without the right to adoption until May 2009), and Portugal (law on limited association without adoption), and the law of homosexual couples without the right of adoption also went into effect in the Swiss canton of Geneva. Laws on civil and registered union were approved and went into effect in the Canadian province of Quebec in 2002 (with joint adoption) and also in Finland in 2002. In that same year, South Africa and Sweden approved the legalization of adoption by same-sex couples with the right to adoption. Same-sex marriage laws were passed and went into effect in Belgium in 2003 (without adoption until April 2006) and in the Canadian provinces of Ontario and British Columbia.

26 Cahill. *Same-sex Marriage in the United States: Focus on the Facts*, 9.

27 Pinello. *America's Struggle for Same-Sex Marriage*, 74-80.

28 Pinello. *America's Struggle for Same-Sex Marriage*, 80-86.

29 Smith. *State and Local Government*, 129.

30 Faderman. *The Gay Revolution: The Story of the Struggle*, 605.

31 *United States v. Windsor, Executor of the Estate of Spyer*, et al, Supreme Court of the United States, 2013, p. 2.

32 Den Otter. *In Defense of Plural Marriage*, 299-230.

33 *United States v. Windsor, Executor of the Estate of Spyer, et al*, Supreme Court of the United States, 2013, p. 2. See also, Mezey, Nancy J., *LGBT Families*, Los Angeles: SAGE, 2015, pp. 55-56.

34 Porterfield. *Jason, Marriage Equality: Obergefell v. Hodges*, 53-102

35 https://www.supremecourt.gov/opinions/16pdf/16-992_868c.pdf

36 European Parliament Resolution of September 12, 1989, on discrimination against transsexuals cf. Recommendation 1117 (1989) on the condition of transsexuals. https://web.archive.org/web/20100408001958/http://tsnews.at.infoseek.co.jp/european_parliament_resolution890912.htm

37   AJ-0028/94. *Resolution on equal rights for homosexuals and lesbians in the EC*, Official
     Journal of the European Communities, No C 61/40, February 28, 1994.
38   AJ-0028/94. *Resolution on equal rights for homosexuals and lesbians in the EC*, Official
     Journal of the European Communities, No C 61/40, February 28, 1994.
39   AJ-0028/94. *Resolution on equal rights for homosexuals and lesbians in the EC*, Official
     Journal of the European Communities, No C 61/40, February 28, 1994.
40   O'Keeffe. *Legal Issues of the Amsterdam Treaty*, 329.
41   Girard. "Negotiating Sexual Rights and Sexual Orientation at the UN," 331.
42   Girard. "Negotiating Sexual Rights and Sexual Orientation at the UN," 340.
43   Girard. "Negotiating Sexual Rights and Sexual Orientation at the UN," 331-341.
44   Girard. "Negotiating Sexual Rights and Sexual Orientation at the UN," 341-344.
45   2006 Joint Statement Third Session of the Human Rights Council Joint Statement.
     H. E. Wegger Chr. Strømmen, Ambassador & Permanent Representative of Norway
     to the United Nations Office in Geneva. Geneva, December 1, 2006. Corrêa, Sonia;
     Petchesky, Rosalind; Parker, Richard, *Sexuality, Health and Human Rights*, (London
     & New York: Routledge: 2008), 233.
46   "UN: General Assembly Statement Affirms Rights for All. 66 States Condemn
     Violations Based on Sexual Orientation and Gender Identity," Human
     Rights Watch, December 18, 2008. https://www.hrw.org/news/2008/12/18/
     un-general-assembly-statement-affirms-rights-all
47   SG/SM/13311-HR/5043, December 10, 2010. https://www.un.org/press/en/2010/
     sgsm13311.doc.htm
48   A/HRC/RES/17/19. Human Rights Council resolution—Human rights, sexual ori-
     entation and gender identity (adopted June 17, 2011). https://www.ohchr.org/EN/
     Issues/Discrimination/Pages/LGBTUNResolutions.aspx
49   A/HRC/19/41. Discriminatory laws and practices and acts of violence against indi-
     viduals based on their sexual orientation and gender identity. Report of the United
     Nations High Commissioner for Human Rights, November 17, 2011.
50   A/HRC/19/41. Discriminatory laws and practices and acts of violence against indi-
     viduals based on their sexual orientation and gender identity. Report of the United
     Nations High Commissioner for Human Rights, November 17, 2011.
51   A/HRC/RES/27/32. Human Rights Council resolution—Human rights, sexual ori-
     entation and gender identity (adopted September 26, 2014). https://www.ohchr.org/
     EN/Issues/Discrimination/Pages/LGBTUNResolutions.aspx
52   A/HRC/RES/32/2. Protection against violence and discrimination based on sexual
     orientation and gender identity (adopted June 30, 2016). https://www.ohchr.org/EN/
     Issues/Discrimination/Pages/LGBTUNResolutions.aspx
53   These countries are, as of April 2019, Austria, Belgium, Denmark, Finland, France,
     Germany, Ireland, Luxembourg, the Netherlands, Malta, Portugal, Spain, and Sweden.
54   Charter of Fundamental Rights of the European Union, 2000/C 364/01, Official
     Journal of the European Communities C 364/1-22, December 18, 2000.

2

The Legal Configuration of Sexual Orientation and Gender Identity in the Legislation of the Autonomous Community of the Basque Country

Andrea Bertomeu Navarro

Researcher-Collaborator of the Legal Clinic for Social Justice of the
University of the Basque Country

INTRODUCTION

The regulation of sexual orientation and gender identity in the Spanish legal system is a relatively recent phenomenon.[1] This phenomenon has been characterized by following a particular channel. From a legal void at the state level,[2] Autonomous Communities have legislated within their competence framework mainly on certain issues related to transsexuality or gender identity.[3] Numerous regional rules have been approved in recent years (twenty-one to date),[4] and various different projects and law proposals are pending approval but have already been processed in the rest of the autonomous parliaments (five at this time).[5]

In this context, the normative dynamic in the Autonomous Community of the Basque Country does not differ from what has been pointed out before, although, as we shall see, it has just partially materialized. Together with the Autonomous Community of Navarre as one of the pioneers to regulate this matter, with the lights and the shadows, the good and the bad, we will try to briefly explain.

REGIONAL REGULATIONS ON SEXUAL ORIENTATION AND GENDER IDENTITY IN THE AUTONOMOUS COMMUNITY OF THE BASQUE COUNTRY

Two regional rules deserve our attention regarding the regulatory framework of the Basque Country: Law 14/2012, of June 28, *on non-discrimination on grounds of gender identity and recognition of rights of transgender people,* and Decree 234/2015, of December 22, *on the administrative documentation of transsexual persons.*

The first of these, Law 14/2012, relies, as in the case of Navarre, on a vision still clinging to a pathological criterion,[6] but it is a more inclusive rule than the Navarre Regional Law. Its article 3 defines transsexual persons not only as those who, in accordance with the provisions of State Law 3/2007, have proceeded or are proceeding to rectify the mention of sex in the Civil Registry, but also as those others who can prove, through a report from a medical or psychological professional staff a) that they lack personality disorders that lead them to error in terms of gender identity, that they express and intend to be recognized, showing a stable, undoubted, and permanent will about it; and b) that present a dissonance, equally stable and persistent, for at least six months, between the biological sex and the gender identity felt.[7]

This choice for a broader[8] concept has not been alien to the controversy. Initially, the Government of the State considered the possibility of filing an appeal of unconstitutionality against this rule, considering that such definition could violate the scope of jurisdiction established in article 149.1.8th of the Spanish Constitution and invade exclusive areas of state legislation. To resolve such conflict, the Bilateral Commission for Cooperation between the Administration of the State and the Administration of the Autonomous Community of the Basque Country began negotiations to resolve such discrepancies, particularly regarding articles 3 and 7 of the Law 14/2012, designating a specific work group for this purpose.[9] These negotiations resulted in a declaration in which both parties agreed to interpret articles 3 and 7 of Law 14/2012 to recognize that a transsexual person included in the Basque Law should be understood exclusively for the purposes of this Law and in the strict scope of the Autonomous Community of the Basque Country, without affecting the legal identity of the interested party, as long as there was no revision of the registration ruled by Law 3/2007, of March 15, *about the rectification of the mention relative to the sex of people.*[10]

Based on this finally agreed-upon definition, which marks the framework of action of the rule, in just eighteen articles, Law 14/2012 projects its protective umbrella mainly to the scope of health (Chapter III), labor (Chapter IV), and education (Chapter V). It includes, in turn, measures against transphobia (article 5), support and counseling measures for transgender people as well as their families and close relatives (article 6), and measures regarding the processing of adequate administrative documentation during the process of sex reassignment (article 7).

According to Chapter II of this Law, public policy on transsexuality must have as a cornerstone the commitment to treat people according to their gender identity, that which corresponds to the sex to which they feel they belong. Administrations should promote a proactive policy regarding the needs of transsexual people. Among them are the creation of information, guidance, and advice services to transsexual people as well as their families and close associates, and the promotion of the defense of their rights. In this sense, what should be understood is the establishment of services such as Berdindu[11] or Ibiltari,[12] dependent on the Family Policy and Diversity Directorate of the Basque Government, although managed by LGTBI+ associations such as Aldarte (Araba and Bizkaia), Gehitu (Gipuzkoa), and Errespetuz (Ibiltari), that constitute real information and attention services of the Basque Government for issues related to sexual and gender diversity; or the Eraberean network, integrated by the Basque Government (also through the Directorate of Family Policy and Diversity) and by various social organizations working in the field of immigration, the Roma people and LGTBI+ groups, whose mission is to ensure equality of treatment and nondiscrimination in public policies and in the civil society of the Basque Country.[13]

Such commitment is made concrete through the referral that the Law itself makes to a regulatory development regarding the issuance of administrative documentation for transsexual persons according to their feelings and to favor a better integration during the aforementioned process, thus avoiding situations of suffering or discrimination. In this regard, in relation to immigrants with residence in the Basque Country, such administrative documentation will remain in force until such time as the registration change in their countries of origin can be made. However, the most remarkable and controversial rule is found in its final paragraph: from the issuance of such documentation, or in any case from the issuance of the National Identity Document that reflects the sex felt by the transsexual person, the Law commits the Basque Government, the regional councils, the local administrations, and any other public bodies belonging to the Basque Autonomous Community to enable all the necessary mechanisms to eliminate from all archives, databases, and other files any reference to the previous identity of the person or any other information that makes their transsexual reality known. This ultimately was, as we already suggested before, the cause of controversy between the Basque Autonomous Community and the Government of the State through a possible appeal of unconstitutionality, because the State understood that the elimination of such data from databases and other files collided with the state competence of management of public records and instruments and with the State Law 3/2007, of March 15, *regulating the rectification registration of the mention relative to the sex of the persons*, which establishes that the constitutive effects will take place as of the inscription in the Civil Registry of the resolution of registry rectification.[14]

As far as the health-care sector is concerned, the Law establishes free diagnosis, hormonal treatments, and plastic-surgical interventions, as well as the rest of the treatments determined necessary to solve the problems derived from a body development that goes against the one corresponding to the gender felt by the person. For this purpose, the creation, through regulation, of a referral unit on transsexuality within the Basque Health System[15] is established within a maximum period of six months from the entry into force of the regulation (article 8.2 and Second Additional Provision), as well as the development of a clinical guide for the care of transsexual people in the field of psychological, medical, surgical, and sexological care (article 9 and First Additional Provision).[16] It guarantees, in turn, the right of transgender people to be treated according to their gender identity, to be informed and consulted about the treatments that affect them, and to be attended by professional staff with sufficient experience regarding both the specific specialty concerned and transsexuality itself.

Foresight about transsexual minors deserves special mention. They have the full right to receive the opportune diagnosis and medical treatment related to their transsexuality, especially regarding hormonal therapy. Such attention, as minors, must be done in accordance with the provisions of Law 3/2005, of February 18, *on care and protection of children and adolescents*, and Law 41/2002, of November 14, *regulating of patient autonomy and rights and obligations in terms of information and clinical documentation.*[17]

In the labor field, the Basque Law is extremely brief, limiting its action to two measures, both excessively general in our opinion. On the one hand, it emphasizes the principle of nondiscrimination on the grounds of gender identity in terms of hiring personnel and in promotion policies, circumscribing it within the framework of the actions of the Basque public administrations themselves and of all those public bodies and entities ascribed or dependent on them. On the other hand, it provides for the preparation and application of positive action plans and measures to favor the recruitment and employment of transsexual persons.

In the field of education, the Law provides for two-way action. Firstly, it ensures that methods, curricula, and educational resources become an appropriate channel to promote understanding and respect for the diversity of gender identities. It ensures, in turn, the training and awareness of both the students and the teaching staff in this regard. Secondly, it encourages the adoption of the necessary measures to protect transsexual students, staff, and teachers from all forms of discrimination, social exclusion, and violence based on gender identity.[18]

Finally, it is necessary to emphasize that the Law states a series of measures against transphobia (article 5). However, they are not accompanied by any sanctioning provision, even of an administrative nature.

The second of the rules that demand our attention is Decree 234/2015 expedites the administrative documentation while transsexual persons await the rectification of their sex in the Civil Registry.

For the purposes of implementing this rule, a first question that arises is the scope of its application. According to article 7 of Law 14/2012, access to said administrative documentation extends to all transsexual persons with "residence" in the Basque Country. According to the Decree, the beneficiaries of such documentation will be the persons with "effective residence" in any of the municipalities of the Basque Country who have the status of transsexual in accordance with Law 14/2012. Despite the apparent discrepancy between both precepts and the potential conflict that this might generate in relation to an exclusive competence of the State regarding matters of nationality, immigration, emigration, aliens, and right to asylum, included in the article 149.1.2ª of the Spanish Constitution, in the light of the agreement adopted within the scope of the Bilateral Commission for Cooperation Administration of the State-Administration of the Autonomous Community of the Basque Country. Immigrants should benefit from such recognition, regardless of their legal or administrative situation.[19] This is on the understanding that such recognition exhausts its effects in the Basque jurisdiction and does not alter the legal status of such persons.

The procedure provided for in the rule must be initiated at the request of the person concerned, by themselves or duly represented, as, in the case of minors, always through their legal representatives (article 4.1). It must be in a standardized model, accompanied by documentation proving the identity of the applicant (DNI, NIE, or any other official document issued in the country of origin); a recent color photograph of their face; the registration certificate of the town hall where they live; and a document proving the initiation before the corresponding Civil Registry of the governmental record of rectification or, in its absence, the medical or psychological report that proves their transsexual condition in accordance with article 3 of Law 14/2012. Once accepted that the person is included in the scope of application of this Decree, the Directorate competent in matters of promotion of real and effective equality in the field of emotional-sexual freedom (Directorate of Family Policy and Diversity) will dictate administrative resolution of granting such documentation. That will consist of a card with the data referred to the applicant, and it will be valid until the registration rectification of the mention regarding sex in the Civil Registry or, in the case of immigrants with residence in the Basque Country, until such time as they can proceed to the registry change in the country of origin. With regard to the effects of such documentation, there are two aspects to be highlighted. The first is the possibility that the interested party instructs to the competent body to issue the documentation that brings this resolution to the attention of the public administrations that it considers should be informed. The second is that the Basque public administrations will be obliged to adopt the administrative and other measures to guarantee that these people are treated according to their freely determined gender identity. In this sense, their right is expressly recognized in the health and educational fields in accordance to their own will regarding their gender identity, to be identified by the corresponding name, and for the administrative documentation to be adapted to it.

THE PENDING NORMATIVE WORK

Current legislation on gender identity in the Basque Country can be welcomed with moderate satisfaction for its pioneering nature. However, it requires a deep revision and update that more adequately responds to the diversity of the LGBTQI+ collective and the difficulties it faces.

The aims should be twofold. Current rules, limited to regulating issues derived from transsexuality and gender identity, should be adapted to comply with the recommendations made by international organizations, mainly in the depathologization of transsexuality referrals, updating the legislative framework to a reality that effectively guarantees the rights of transgender people and, in particular, the self-determination of gender. It is also essential to address more completely the issues of identity, gender expression, and all those related to the affective-sexual orientation to address the lack of comprehensive and real public programming that encompass public administrations of the Basque Autonomous Community (in the municipal, provincial, and regional framework). This applies to each and every one of the areas in which the rights of the LGBTQI+ collective are still in need of protection (among others: education, health, work, family, leisure and culture, sports, and international cooperation on the much-needed fight against hate crimes). International hate crimes in 2018 saw a recovery of 21.8 percent on sexual orientation and gender identity, exceeding the state average by 11 points. In this sense, sadly, the Basque Country is last among Autonomous Communities in Spain and is one of the last to face the task of developing a comprehensive LGTBI+ Law.[20]

Facing this reality, however, we should positively note that, at the time of this writing, several initiatives are under way to achieve such comprehensiveness in the regulation of sexual orientation and gender identity referrals. Some of them are still in an embryonic stage. Let's give a brief account of them:

In relation to a possible reform of the aforementioned Law 14/2012, the Chrysallis Euskal Herria[21] and Errespetuz[22] associations presented in 2018 before the parliamentary groups of the Basque Legislative Chamber a *draft of a law project for the recognition of the rights of transsexual people.* This draft addresses the reform of the aforementioned law from a comprehensive perspective with attention to transgender people in all areas. Thus, throughout its seventy-five articles, measures are addressed in areas already provided for in the current law, such as health (Chapter I), education (Chapter III), and labor (Chapter IV), with greater depth and detail. They include new areas, such as family (Chapter II); relative (Chapter V); youth and the elderly (Chapter VI); leisure, culture, and sports (Chapter VI); security, justice, and emergencies (Chapter IX); and infractions and sanctions (Chapter XIV). Two of the most remarkable elements of this draft are found in its General Provisions: The scope of application extends to any transsexual person, regardless of age, nationality, domicile or residence, which is located or acts in the territorial scope of the Basque Country (article 3). And the transsexual person is defined as one who expresses that the sex incorrectly placed at birth regarding the genitals does not correspond to their sexual identity; for which it will be enough for the concerned people to express their felt gender identity, not any report or accreditation, neither medical, nor psychological, nor of any other type (article 4).

The second of the initiatives refers to a process rather than a legislative document in itself. Thus, a significant number of associations and LGBTQI+ entities of the Basque Autonomous Community have launched, together with the Legal Clinic for Social Justice of the University of the Basque Country, a process that aims to jointly develop a comprehensive LGBTQI+ Basque Bill to present before the legislative body, as well as the creation of a Basque Observatory against LGBTQI+ phobia. Despite being in the early stages, this initiative has created a working forum whose outcomes, not even being possible to glimpse, are allowing the exchange of diverse points of view that, without any doubt, will enrich the possible final result.

I do not want to end this text without mentioning an area that different associations and LGBTQI+ entities have been emphasizing in recent times, as evidenced by the many works entrusted to the analysis of the situation of the people who make up this part of the collective.[23] I refer to LGBTQI+ people who are migrants and applicants for international protection, who bear the burden of a multiplicity of vulnerabilities that make them require special protection. Being aware that the exclusive competence in matters of immigration and asylum belongs to the Government of the State, the authorities of the Basque Autonomous Community, and its Parliament must consider such appeals and extend the protective umbrella of the rules to the members of the LGBTQI+ collective who suffer most from the lack of protection.

BIBLIOGRAPHY

Alventosa del Rio, Josefina. *Discriminación por orientación sexual e identidad de género en el derecho español.* Madrid: Ministerio de Trabajo y Asuntos Sociales. Subdirección General de Información Administrativa y Publicaciones, 2008.

———. "La regulación de la identidad de género en las comunidades autónomas," *Actualidad Jurídica Iberoamericana*, no. 2 (February 2015): 745-60.

Belsué Guillorme, Katrina. "Sexo, género y transexualidad: de los desafíos teóricos a las debilidades de la legislación española," *Acciones e Investigaciones Sociales*, no. 29 (July 2011): 7-32.

Bertomeu Navarro, Andrea. *Realidad jurídico-social de las personas LGBTI+ solicitantes y beneficiarias de protección internacional en la CAPV.* Donostia: Gehitu, 2019.

Bustos Moreno, Yolanda. *La transexualidad* (de acuerdo a la Ley 3/2007, de 15 de marzo). Madrid: Dykinson, 2008.

Imaz Zubiaur, Leire. "La libre determinación de la identidad de género como derecho funda-mental. Normativa internacional, europea, estatal y autonómica." *Justicia en tiempos de crisis*, directed by Ixusko Ordeñana Geruzaga and Maite Uriarte Ricote, 565-605. Bilbao. Servicio editorial de la Universidad del País Vasco, 2016.

Mújica, Lala. *El bullying y la violencia hacia el colectivo LGTBI+en el ámbito de la educación no formal.* Bilbao: Aldarte, 2016.

Olartua, Elena y Villar Amparo. *Gays, Lesbianas y Transexuales: reflexiones para una buena acogida.* Bilbao: Aldarte, 2009

Platero Méndez, Raquel. "Transexualidad y agenda política: una historia de (dis)continui-dades y patologización." *Política y Sociedad*, vol. 46, no. 1-2 (2009): 107-128.

NOTES

1   Josefina Alventosa del Rio. *Discriminación por orientación sexual e identidad de género en el derecho español* (Madrid: Ministerio de Trabajo y Asuntos Sociales. Subdirección General de Información Administrativa y Publicaciones, 2008); Katrina Belsué Guillorme, "Sexo, género y transexualidad: de los desafíos teóricos a las debilidades de la legislación española," Acciones e Investigaciones Sociales, no. 29 (July 2011): 7-32.

2   Apart from the normative milestones that constitute Law 13/2005, of July 1, by which the Civil Code is modified in the matter of the right to marry (BOE, no. 157, July 2, 2005) and Law 3/2007, of March 15, regulating in the matter of the registry rec-tification of the mention regarding the sex of the people (BOE, no. 3/2007, March 16, 2007), at the time of writing four proposals of law have been introduced in the Spanish legislative chambers: a Proposition of law for the reform of Law 3/2007, of March 15, regulating the registry rectification of the mention relative to the sex of the persons, to allow the registry rectification of the mention relative to the sex and name of the minors transsexual and/or trans, to modify the requirements established in article 4 regarding the registration of sex change, and to enable measures to im-prove the integration of foreigners residing in Spain (122/000072); a Proposition of law on the legal protection of trans people and the right to self-determination of sexual identity and expression of gender (122/000191); a Proposition of law amend-ing Law 19/2007, of July 11, against violence, racism, xenophobia, and intolerance in sport, to eradicate homophobia, biphobia, and transphobia (622/000004); and, fi-nally, a Proposition of law against discrimination based on sexual orientation, iden-tity, or expression of gender and sexual characteristics, and social equality of lesbian, gay, bisexual, transgender, transgender, and intersex (122/000097). Raquel Platero Méndez, "Transexualidad y agenda política: una historia de (dis)continuidades y pa-tologización." *Política y Sociedad*, 46, no. 1-2 (2009), 107-128.

3   Josefina Alventosa del Rio. "La regulación de la identidad de genero en las comuni-dades autónomas," *Actualidad Jurídica Iberoamericana*, no. 2 (February 2015): 745-60.

4   Among the regional laws currently in force, we can mention the cases of Andalusia (2), Aragon (2), Balearic Islands (2), Canary Islands (1), Catalonia (2), Valencian Community (2), Estremadura (2), Galicia (1), Madrid (2), Murcia (1), Navarre (2), and Basque Country (2).

5 Among the bills and legislative proposals currently under way in the regional chambers, it is worth mentioning the cases of Asturias (Draft bill of the Principality of Asturias guaranteeing the right to free expression of sexual and/or gender identity), Cantabria (Draft Law of Cantabria guaranteeing the rights of lesbian, gay, trans, transgender, bisexual and intersex persons and nondiscrimination based on sexual orientation and gender identity, number 9L/1000-0027), Castilla-La Mancha (Proposed Law of Social Equality, treatment and nondiscrimination for sexual orientation and gender identity in Castilla-La Mancha, presented by the Parliamentary Group Podemos, file 09/PPL-00022), Castilla y León (Proposed Law of Social Equality of Sexual and Gender Diversity, and Public Policies against discrimination based on sexual orientation and gender identity of the Community of Castilla y León, presented to Parliamentary Groups in Castilla y León, Socialist, Citizens, and Mixed), and La Rioja (Proposition of Equality Law, recognition of gender identity and rights of transgender people).

6 Although throughout its lengthy preamble there are constant references to the necessary overcoming of such a pathological vision and its unwanted consequences in relation to the violation of the most fundamental rights of transsexual people (up to five of the twenty-three paragraphs that make up his statement of reasons refer to it), the text does not dispense with such conception in the end. Leire Imaz Zubiaur, "La libre determinación de la identidad de género como derecho fundamental. Normativa internacional, europea, estatal y autonómica." in *Justicia en tiempos de crisis,* directed by Ixusko Ordeñana Geruzaga and Maite Uriarte Ricote (Bilbao: Servicio editorial de la Universidad del País Vasco, 2016), 565-605.

7 Yolanda Bustos Moreno, *La transexualidad* (de acuerdo a la Ley 3/2007, de 15 de marzo) (Dykinson: Madrid, 2008).

8 Despite adopting a broader concept than its predecessor, the law of Navarre, the Basque Law does not reach the height of the Andalusian Law 2/2014 that defines gender identity, in its article 3, as "the internal and individual experience of the gender and how each person feels it, which may or may not correspond to the sex assigned at birth, and which includes the personal experience of the body. It may involve the modification of appearance or bodily function through pharmacological, surgical or other means, provided that this is freely chosen" and establishes the right to gender self-determination (article 2).

9 This is in relation to this broader concept recognized by the Basque Law, RESOLUTION of October 11, 2012, of the General Secretariat of Autonomous and Local Coordination, which publishes the Agreement of the Bilateral Commission of Cooperation Administration of the State-Administration of the Autonomous Community of the Basque Country in relation to the Basque Country Law 14/2012, of June 28, on non-discrimination for reasons of gender identity and recognition of the rights of transsexual persons (BOE, no. 261, of October 30, 2012) and RESOLUTION of September 25, 2012, of the Secretary General of the Presidency, which provides for the publication of the Agreement of the Bilateral Commission for Cooperation Administration of the State-Administration of the Autonomous Community of the Basque Country, in relation to the Law of the Basque Country

14/2012, of June 28, of nondiscrimination for reasons of gender identity and recognition of the rights of the person as transsexuals (BOPV, no. 210, of October 30, 2012).

10 RESOLUTION of March 27, 2013, of the Deputy Minister of the Legal System, which provides for the publication of the Agreement of the Bilateral Cooperation Commission Administration of the State-Administration of the Autonomous Community of the Basque Country in relation to articles 3 and 7 of Law 14/2012, of June 28, on nondiscrimination for reasons of gender identity and recognition of the rights of transgender people.

11 The Berdindu service offers information and assistance to lesbian, gay, trans, bisexual, and intersex people as well as their family and associates. At the same time, it offers information and attention to the educational community, to the different social and professional agents, to the media and society in general with the aim of eliminating homophobia (http://www.euskadi.eus/gobierno-vasco/berdindu/)

12 The Ibiltari service offers itinerant attention to trans people that facilitates the user who wishes to be treated in their place of residence. It is a service based on "peer attention," meaning all users of the service are served by a trans person with their same sexual identity.

13 The Eraberean network offers a specialized care service, which consists of assistance and advice to possible victims of discrimination based on racial, ethnic, or national origin and sexual orientation or identity and gender identity, and to people who know discriminatory situations. In addition to offering assistance to people in specific situations, the Eraberean network works with a preventive, awareness, and social awareness approach. To this end, it conducts awareness-raising activities, agent training, creation of outreach materials, advice to institutions, and social organizations. The associations that make up the Eraberean network are: Aldarte, CEAR Euskadi, Cruz Roja, Gao Lacho Drom, CITE-CC.OO Bizkaia, Errespetuz, Kale Dor Kayiko, Nevipen, AGIFUGI, Gehitu y SOS Racismo Gipuzkoa. http://www.euskadi.eus/gobierno-vasco/eraberean/

14 Article 5.1 of Law 3/2007. See also, Instruction, of October 23, 2018, of the General Directorate of Registries and Notaries, on change of name in the Civil Registry of transsexual persons. BOE, no. 257, of October 24, 2018.

15 The Gender Identity Unit (UIG), reference unit for the entire Basque Country in the field, was created in 2009 at the University Hospital of Cruces to cover the health needs of transgender people, with a multidisciplinary perspective: psychiatry, psychology, endocrinology. and plastic and reconstructive surgery. According to the data presented by the heads of the unit in the Basque Parliament, from its implementation until 2017, the Gender Identity Unit had attended a total of 237 people, fifty of whom were minors. There were 4,870 outpatient consultations during this time, and 134 surgeries were recorded.

16 In response to the mandate established by law, the Basque Government published the "Guía de atención integral a las personas en situación de transexualidad" in 2016. Document available in: http://www.euskadi.eus/contenidos/informacion/guia_transexualidad/es_def/adjuntos/guia_transexuales_cs.pdf

17 BOE, no. 274, of November 15, 2002.

18 Gobierno Vasco. Protocolo para los centros educativos en el acompañamiento al alumnado trans o con comportamiento de género no normativo y sus familias (http://www.gizartelan.ejgv.euskadi.eus/aa38aLGTBWar/recursos/content-Viewer/9129?R01HNoPortal=true); Fundación EDE, Departamentos de Empleo y Políticas Sociales, Gobierno Vasco. *Lesbofobia, Homofobia y Transfobia en el sistema educativo*, un acercamiento cualitativo, 2016 (http://www.gizartelan.ejgv.euskadi.eus/contenidos/informacion/28junio_diainternacional/es_documen/adjuntos/InformeLGTBfobia.pdf); Lala Mújica. El bullying y la violencia hacia el colectivo LGTBI+en el ámbito de la educación no formal (Bilbao: Aldarte, 2016).

19 Alventosa del Rio, Josefina. "La regulación de la identidad de género en las comunidades autónomas," Actualidad Jurídica Iberoamericana, no. 2 (February 2015): 752-53.

20 Eleven Autonomous Communities have approved a comprehensive LGTBI+ Law: Andalusia, Aragon, Balearic Islands, Cantabria, Catalonia, Valencia, Estremadura, Galicia, Madrid, Murcia, and Navarre.

21 Chrysallis Euskal Herria is an association of families of transsexual minors from Araba, Bizkaia, Gipuzkoa, and Navarre (https://chrysallis.org.es/tag/chrysallis-euskal-herria/) that from the end of 2018 will be called Naizen (https://naizen.eus/) when leaving the state association Chrysallis.

22 Errespetuz. Basque Association for the Defense and Integration of Transsexual Persons.

23 Andrea Bertomeu Navarro. *Realidad jurídico-social de las personas LGBTI+ solicitantes y beneficiarias de protección internacional en la CAPV* (Donostia: GEHITU, 2019); Elena Olartua y Amparo Villar. *Gays, Lesbianas y Transexuales: reflexiones para una buena acogida* (Bilbao: ALDARTE, 2009); Inmaculada Mujika Flores (Contenidos); Amparo Villar Sáenz (Coord.). *Lesbianas: derecho de asilo para las mujeres perseguidas por motivos de orientación sexual* (Bilbao: Aldarte, 2006);

3

Queer Discourses and Practices in the Basque Feminist Movement

María Ruiz Torrado[1]
University of the Basque Country, EHU

When, to the shout of *feminism will be transfeminist[2] or it will not be*, feminists were asked directly in State Feminist Sessions in Granada (2009), probably few of them imagined the broad scope that queer approaches would end up having in feminist collectives in the Spanish state. There were some notable antecedents: the growth of radical lesbian and gay collectives in the first half of the 1990s,[3] the use of the term "transfeminist" in some presentations at the earlier State Feminist Sessions in Córdoba (2000), and the emergence of a strong movement against pathologizing trans people after 2008. Despite these precedents, queer feminism was not consolidated until that public appearance in Granada.[4]

In the specific context of the Basque Country, queer approaches were developed at different encounters and sessions at least from 2004. Thus, when the Sixth Feminist Sessions of the Basque Country were held (Portugalete, Bizkaia) in April 2008, a radical feminist group began to point toward a new current within feminism. The Medeak collective from Donostia-San Sebastián defended the importance of attacking heteronormativity and centrality of lesbian demands—lesbianism was not on the Basque feminist movement's political agenda—while inviting people to reflect on the political subject of feminism.[5] A year later, members of Medeak attended the Granada Sessions, adhering, alongside other Basque feminist groups such as Garaipen, EHGAM and 7menos20, to the *Manifiesto para la insurrección transfeminista* (Manifesto for transfeminist insurrection, 2009). This manifesto, signed by diverse collectives and activists close to transfeminism in the Spanish state, reaffirmed a new feminist perspective, different from that of "classic" feminism based on gender binarism and *women* as the only political subject.[6]

> We no longer have to be only women. The political subject of feminism "women" has become too restricted, it is exclusive in itself, it leaves out the dykes, the trans, prostitutes, those of the veil, those who don't earn a lot and don't go to college, those that shout, those without any papers, the queens . . .
>
> Let's destroy the gender and sex binomial as a political practice. [. . .] let's continue to unmask the structures of power, division and hierarchy. If we do not learn that the man/woman difference is a cultural production, just like the hierarchical structure that oppresses us, we will reinforce the structure that tyrannizes us: the man/woman borders. We all produce gender, let us all produce freedom. Let us argue with infinite genders . . .[7]

From 2010 on, and thanks to later encounters, sessions, and assemblies, the transfeminist movement managed to articulate itself definitively, both in the Spanish state and in the Basque Country.[8] In the Basque context specifically, diverse feminist collectives immersed themselves in queer discourses and practices, giving rise to interesting transfeminist contributions. From our current perspective, looking back, we can affirm that queer feminist approaches have been disseminated broadly and received widely, leading to remarkable transformations in the Basque feminist movement, although not exempt from criticism and debate. This requires a more detailed analysis of what the queer perspective has contributed to Basque feminist groups at a theoretical and practical level, but without forgetting the existing tensions and divergences among different feminist positions. I will try to carry out this analysis in the following pages.

In the first section, I will undertake a brief theoretical approach to the origins and development of the movement and queer theory, also exploring some discrepancies between "classical" feminist approaches and queer feminist approaches. In the following three sections, based mainly on the information gathered in four in-depth interviews with activists from different queer feminist collectives, I will delve more deeply into the queer discourses and practices that have developed within the Basque feminist movement, also addressing the disagreements among different groups.

QUEER MOVEMENTS, THEORIES, AND (DIS)ENCOUNTERS

The first manifestations of what we now call the "queer movement" occurred in the context of certain social and political struggles that emerged in the second half of the 1980s, principally in the United States, but also in some European countries. Three major crises coincided at that time, leading to the formation of queer activism: the AIDS crisis; the crisis of heterocentric, white, and bourgeois feminism; and the cultural crisis stemming from the assimilation by the capitalist system of the incipient gay subculture.[9] As a catalyst for social protest, the convergence of these three crises led to the birth of the queer movement, in the streets, in the hands of people who were at the margins or on the periphery of hegemonic gender models. Through their actions, those early queer activists questioned the prevailing gender system, trying to veto dominant discourses and reclaiming a position of resistance. From the start they were fully aware that their bodies were "political," bodies susceptible to being violently interpellated and, in turn, bodies-resistance against the regulations.[10] On the basis of these reflections, they decided to transform their situation of social vulnerability into a position from which to respond to gender impositions; and, for this, they backed terming themselves "queer."

In the English-speaking context, "queer" is an umbrella term that attempts to encompass diverse gender dissidences, that is, diverse border or peripheral positions at the margins of dominant gender models. Nevertheless, if one consults a dictionary, we see that the term has many other meanings:

> **queer** • **adj.** **1** strange; odd. Brit. informal, dated slightly ill. **2** informal, derogatory (of a man) homosexual. • **n.** informal, derogatory a homosexual man. • **v.** informal spoil or ruin. – PHRASES **in Queer Street** Brit. Informal, dated in difficulty or debt. **queer someone's pitch** Brit. Spoil someone's plans or chances of doing something.[11]

In reality, "queer" is an old and polysemic word that has evolved over the years, acquiring different meanings, but it is obvious that many of those meanings are offensive or pejorative.[12] It can be an insult or a derogatory word full of stigmatization to mock homosexual people or refer in general to what does not correspond to the norm, to what is unusual or deviant. However, queer activism has used this concept as a self-appointed strategy to preempt insults. Thus, those who have been the attempted targets of insult with that word have appropriated it and have used it as a vindication of their "deviant" being, attempting to achieve a kind of boomerang effect.

The first mention of queer activism can be found in street pamphlets in New York, Chicago, San Francisco, and London. From 1990 on, numerous groups were created: Queer Nation and ACT UP (AIDS Coalition to Unleash Power) in the United States; OutRage, Whores of Babylon, SISSY (Schools Information Services on Sexuality), and PUSSY (Perverts Undermining State Scrutiny) in England, for example. With a generally rather provocative language, they began, as noted, to call themselves "queer." According to an anonymous pamphlet distributed under the title of *Queer Power Now* (1991) in London, "queer means to fuck with gender. There are straight queers, bi-queers, tranny queers, lez queers, fag queers, SM queers, fisting queers."[13] Inspired by forms of protest in feminist collectives, black groups, and civic movements, those first queer groups conducted quite potent activities: getting in and demonstrating in AZT-producing laboratories,[14] whose price was exorbitant for people suffering from AIDS; organizing patrols to keep watch over sexual contact areas; and kissing one another publicly in shopping centers at rush hour.

The people who claimed to be "queer" thus started to demand "telling it themselves" with their own discourses and representations.[15] They resisted being classified according to normative gender classifications, rejecting any kind of attempt to regulate or assimilate them. Likewise, they were encouraged to re-examine the interrelationships between gender, sex, sexuality, and power, creating new approaches to topics such as desire and identity.[16] Following somewhat postmodern perspectives, its main ideological bases have been a critique of gender binarism; the deconstruction of the naturalization of sex, sexuality, and identity; the questioning of the heterosexual norm; and the deconstruction of rigid and immovable perspectives on the identifications and expressions of gender.

Shortly after these ideological approaches emerged in the streets and the first queer social revolts began, the academy began to develop theories. Some lesbian intellectuals in the American university context, such as Teresa de Lauretis[17] and Judith Butler,[18] who had been committed to the feminist movement and the struggle against lesbo-trans-homophobia, began a theoretical reflection based on questionings that were being addressed in the queer movement. This theoretical reflection has developed to make up what we now know as "queer theory." It is not at all easy to explain queer theory. It does not imply a coherent finished theoretical corpus, but rather a set of diverse theoretical contributions, not free of contradictions.[19] But, by way of approximation, most queer theoretical contributions share the following key characteristics:

> Drawing on post-structuralist theories to examine power relations relating to sex, sexuality & gender . . . through destabilizing the taken-for-granted dominant understanding which assumes that heterosexuality is the normal or natural standard of sexuality, and categorizes people in relation to this by . . . exposing how sexual and gender identities are constructed through the available ways of thinking and being in different times & places; performed: some-thing that we do rather than something that we (essentially) are.[20]

In recent years, these ideas have achieved great significance, beyond just that within the queer movement and theory, but also in the protest prac-tices and the theorizations of feminist activism. This has led to the emer-gence of some tension, stemming from agreements and disagreements, affinities and divergences, between different perspectives. These tensions have mainly revolved around three questions: the postmodern character of queer approaches, the debate about who makes up the political subject of feminism, and the relationship between feminism and queer thinking.

With regard to the postmodern character of queer approaches, some feminists have questioned whether a critical movement or postmodern political activism of any kind is viable. Seyla Benhabib, for example, believes that there is a compatibility problem, because the very essence of postmodernity—which she defines as adherence to three theses: the death of Man, the death of History, and the death of Metaphysics—could invalidate feminism.[21] According to this author, from a postmod-ern position, we could neither criticize androcentrism, nor denounce gender inequalities, just as we could not address the social, economic, political, and symbolic constitution of human differences. However, some feminists, on the contrary, believe in the existence of points of affinity between feminism and postmodernity. With regard to the debate about the political subject of feminism, the tensions derive from the fact that queer feminist perspectives defend covering a multiplic-ity of subjects, in addition to just "women." There are feminist posi-tions that have understood this as a loss—or even as an attack—and have pointed out the danger of not giving sufficient importance to the specific inequalities suffered by women. In the same vein, the relation-ship between feminism and queer thinking has also been debated, since there are feminists who believe that an activism that does not focus exclusively on women, or that questions the category *women*, cannot be considered "feminism." Feminists who work from queer perspectives, however, affirm that they have not renounced or gone beyond feminism, despite not denying that they are immersed in a different kind of femi-nism. These tensions, to some extent, continue to apply today.

QUEER DISCOURSES IN BASQUE FEMINIST COLLECTIVES
Following a brief theoretical consideration of the origins and the development of queer approaches, in this section we will begin to explore more deeply what the nonbinary perspective has implied in the Basque feminist movement, through an analysis of the informa-tion obtained in four in-depth interviews with activists from diverse queer feminist collectives. Specifically, we will examine different aspects related to their discourses.

Starting with their general theoretical approaches, the people inter-viewed claim to have come to a queer perspective based on various more or less similar theoretical references. Among their sources of information are individuals and specific groups, with whom they have a relationship and affinity for sharing a similar ideological position. But, at the same time, the many theoretical readings they make, mainly from the works of radical feminist authors linked to the queer theory, are also notable.

> When we started to get together, that was when we started to interact with other groups, with Medeak for example, since Medeak had been working on that for some time, they had more of a discourse . . . We started with them. Then, each one of us has been reading, who has been able to, [Judith] Butler [*Laughter*], Monique Wittig, texts out there, you go online, the internet . . . Then there are the talks. Particularly with Sejo [Carrascosa], I have learned a lot. LETICIA[22]

The people interviewed believe that their influences, references, and ideas coincide clearly with queer approaches, but it is important to note that in general they do not usually use this concept. It seems to them that, in the Basque context, it is too much of an academic term and that in the street it does not have the strength it should, because people do not know what it means. Thus, they prefer terms that in our surroundings are known and have a similar impact.

> We're queer because we've been influenced by queer theory, by queer actions. The word "queer" was at the beginning fundamental for us, but it is a matter of translation. We don't think the translation is good. At the state level or in the Basque Country, if you tell someone "I'm queer," "What? What is that . . . ?" If you tell someone in English "I'm queer," you're saying something very different. Then, you have to look for that game. What you can't do is translate the word, and not the concept. [. . .] At university you're "queer" because of Judith Butler and I don't know what, but in other areas no. You're a "*bollera,*"[23] you're a "*marica.*"[24] ITU[25]

One of the approaches they emphasize the most is the critique of binary and dichotomous gender perspectives, to the point of estimating that it is one of the keys or specific characteristics of its movement. Along those lines, great importance is attached to understanding that both gender and sex are social and historical constructions, which must be deconstructed and given new meaning. They criticize any attempt at biological determinism, since they argue that our physical characteristics should not limit us or force us into anything, with regard to our identity and gender expression. Likewise, they often mention trans and intersex people as examples that show the flawed nature of gender binary schemes, stating that we cannot limit ourselves to just two gender models. They try to understand gender as performance, as something that we "do," and not something that "we are," so that each person can freely decide how to situate themselves in the world.

Another issue that appears frequently in the interviews is that of the critique of heteronormativity. The people interviewed are against the presumption and the imposition of being heterosexual. They want to put an end to the idea that there are good and bad, normal and abnormal, natural and unnatural sexualities, and also aim to end the privileges and punishments implied by some sexualities or others (image 1).

Likewise, they harshly criticize structures and power relations in general. On the one hand, they address the discriminations suffered by people who are outside the dominant gender models; and, on the other, they deal with the discrimination suffered by women in relation to men. Yet in dealing with these inequalities, they try not to forget the different forms of

IMAGE 1. Banner of the TransMarikaBollo Koordinadora Feminista from Donostia-San Sebastián demanding the right to sexual freedom (Source: María Ruiz Torrado).

oppression that also exist in terms of categorization axes such as social class, race/ethnicity, and nationality. The people interviewed say they want to dismantle any type of hierarchy, so they have chosen to identify their activism with "the margins," and thus be able to defend options that until now have been excluded and marginalized. In the context of their struggle against hierarchical and asymmetric relations, they perceive the issue of violence as central. They aim to broaden the concept of sexist violence to encompass both sexist violence against women and trans-homo-lesbophobia.

According to the people interviewed, the main objective of queer feminist collectives is, through revolutionary and transformative activism, to destroy normative gender models. They seek to end the heteropatriarchy and build a plural feminist society, which is also anti-class, anti-capitalist, and anti-racist. However, the people interviewed are aware that this is a really complicated and difficult change.

> We must put an end to the structures, with the system itself as it is made up, at the economic, social, political level, and whatever you want. The thing is that the economic and social order is shit, and you have to break it. [...] Each group and each collective will do what we can. We are not going to change the world either, but to know that the issue is not to improve this a bit, as if the system were good, as if it were a small weakness of the system. No, the system is crap, and you have to change it. Another thing is whether we can do it . . . But you have to know that the objective is the whole system. BEA[26]

From their position of absolute rejection of the current heteropatri-archal system, feminists with a queer position reject assimilation or inte-gration into that system. They say they do not want to be accomplices of such a society, nor do they want to become "normal" for the system, since the options that have been excluded so far are also worthy and legitimate.

> We don't want to be normal, because that always implies hierar-chies, and because it creates discriminations in an order. There is talk of normalization, assimilation . . . "No, the thing is that there is a moment when we do not want you to assimilate us. We want this to change. I don't want you to tell me that I can get married, like you." The thing is, maybe I want to generate other types of relationships. Itu

In the context of the critiques that queer feminism makes of the system, it is possible to find reproaches aimed at specific social insti-tutions. The people interviewed, for example, launch harsh critiques of religions—especially against the Catholic religion—the medical system, and the institutions of the state. They believe that they are the ones that sustain to a large extent the pillars of our gender system.

> The target we should focus on, where I aim for, is largely reli-gion. [. . .] Let's open the sack, open the chests, open the sacred books, and realize that what they contain are not texts that speak of freedom; they are texts that deny freedom. [. . .] The activism with which I feel implicated and involved is that which takes into consideration the need to break these stigmas, or with those actual pains or those real powers, with the patriarchal order, male power, the moral presence of all religions and especially the Judeo-Christian religion. Mikel[27]

Another of the most important discursive characteristics of queer feminism is related to the idea of the fluidity of identity, since they understand "identity" as a flexible, changing, and dynamic social artifice. Thus, they have shown a certain tendency to try to escape rigid, strict, or limiting categorizations, and have sometimes come to be defined as "undefined," "multiple," or "hybrid." However, they admit that some cat-egories are necessary; for that reason they advocate using certain labels, but always in a fluid way, problematizing them. For example, one of the interviewees, Itu, says that in most cases she does not feel like a "woman" because she does not comply with the normative gender model. She says she identifies herself as a woman only at times, and mainly within feminist activism, but in the rest of the situations she prefers to define herself as "transgender."

On a more collective level, some of the queer feminist groups have chosen to name themselves, in addition to "feminist," as "lesbian," "lesbianist," or "dyke." They put this forward as a strategic position that places them, in their opinion, outside the heteronormative logic. In general, the collectives of the people interviewed are reviewing many concepts, and have been inclined to embrace labels of invisible subjects—dykes, queers, whores, migrants, trans . . . The labels sometimes have to do with what they are directly and other times not, but without wanting in any case to take the place of or represent anyone.

According to the people interviewed, in their groups they give great importance to the content of the discourses, but also to the form; that is, they care a lot about language, the way they express themselves, the words they use. Many activists believe that they have a language of their own whose main characteristic is that of being radical, provocative, and politically incorrect. That seditious nature is easily noticeable in some of the slogans that they shout in protests. Among others: "I am a dyke/poof because I like it and I want it." "If my campiness bothers you, it'll be for some reason." "There are poof on balconies too, there are dykes on pavements too." "We are beautiful, we are clever, we are feminist bitches." In this context, self-advocacy strategies, aiming to reclassify words with a derogatory sense, also stand out.

> I believe that we are rescuing terms that have been absolutely pejorative, that in some way we are trying to rescue them and, while the content remains the same, give them a value. "If you say it to insult me, I'll say it as a reason for pride, as something good." [. . .] I think it's a strategy, I don't know whether of an attack, but it's a very good defense. It has to do, I believe, with that liberating approach that queer theory has for me. "I am this, and so what?" And in the face of "I'm this, so what?", usually the other person who wants to hurt you or harm you or underestimate you is left without strategies. Bea

Feminist collectives that employ queer approaches have also dared to create new words, as well as to put into practice oral and written formulas to break free from binary gender schemes. That creative and artistic character of queer feminist groups, as well as in language, can also be seen in the practices they undertake.

QUEER PRACTICES IN BASQUE FEMINIST COLLECTIVES

Exploring more deeply the activities that queer feminist groups conduct in the Basque context, it is noteworthy that in general they attach great importance to political activism. They usually value their participation in feminism as a very positive experience, which is enriching both personally and collectively, and highlight its transforming potential.

> Activism, said in a beautiful way, would be a palette of colors. Each and every one of us knows the intensity of the color tone we have placed. Sometimes, many of us coincide in the same colors, in different intensities ... Let's say that it is a factory producing a transformation of colors in ourselves that each of us then wears as we can, giving it the importance we can, and with the collective tools we possess as a society. [...] For me, I think activism is about dedicating a specific time to certain people, from the first person, from your experience, from your own fantasies, from your own illusions, to transform, to modify those realities that you are aware are obstacles to your happiness. MIKEL

According to the information gathered through the interviews, queer feminists believe that their activism has two main characteristics. On the one hand, they emphasize the importance attached to the personal experiences of each activist. They believe that sharing their experiences, listening, accompanying each other and, in short, building an activism based on affective ties are fundamental for them. On the other, they emphasize their way of combining political protest and fun, through activities that are both ludic and political, to bring to the streets struggle and joy, demands and irony, protest and a sense of humor. With regard to the way of organizing themselves, in general they are small groups with a fairly informal functioning.

> Ours is a total anarchy! [*Laughs*] We don't function ... I mean, we don't have weekly meetings, or "You do that, and I'll do the other thing." It's more like: "What? Shall we get together? What are we going to do? I can do this, what can you do?" We function like that, whatever you do, you want to do it. For me, if you order me to

do something, it's because I don't feel like doing it, because that's what I already work for. We look for things that we enjoy [. . .]. There are also external people. There are now four, five of us now. So, often nearby people collaborate with you, have an idea, give it to you . . . It's more like that. LETICIA

Usually, they do not hold weekly meetings, and many issues are addressed via email or social networks to make it faster and more convenient. When they get together, they organize the tasks they have; they contend that for this, mutual trust is fundamental. They say that, in principle, each activist is in charge of the occupations that they want, assuming also the responsibilities that they feel suitable. There are and they accept different rhythms and levels of involvement, according to the wishes of each member of the group. They think that respecting that is essential for the collective to function properly.

Some of the people interviewed also say that their activism is based on small units, on multiple and diverse guerrilla bands that are in contact and work in different areas, but with a common goal. They believe that being in contact with other groups is really important, and they value the results of the alliances they have maintained or maintain with other groups. They argue that, as with the internal relationships within each group, mutual trust is also basic in external relations.

I think that there is a lot of political and personal trust, and that is important. If there is something that has upset some group, or that has happened to someone, and requires the support of the other groups, you don't question it. That trust is lacking in other areas. [. . .] Although we're very different, we have many points in common. BEA

The groups of people interviewed maintain alliances and contacts with groups in different contexts. The most intense relationships are those with groups that are closest geographically, that is, with those who work in the same city or province, or those who work at the level of the Basque Country. As an example, we can mention the TransMarikaBollo Koordinadora Feminista of Donostia-San Sebastián, created in 2009, and made up of various feminist groups involved in the struggle against heteronormativity and in favor of sexual liberation.[28] However, we must also bear in mind that queer feminist groups maintain relations at the state or international level. A good example is the major involvement of those interviewed in the *Stop Trans Pathologization* global campaign.

With regard to specific dissent, protest, and experimental practices conducted by the groups of people interviewed, it is noteworthy that they are trying to give shape to a powerful, provocative, and politically non-correct street activism that does not leave anyone indifferent. One of its most notable characteristics is the importance given to the corporeal dimension. As we will see below, they undertake many practices in which the body is key, since they understand that our bodies make up the form in which we have to be in the world, so that the corporeal experience must be addressed as a fundamental axis of activism.

Performances are one of the most characteristic practices of queer feminist collectives. They are staged shows in which diverse subjects are approached, like power relations and sexist violence, and which give a lot of importance to the symbolic aspect. For example, in such representa-tions, ropes have been used as a symbol of union and dependence at the same time, huge penises as a symbol of patriarchy, and bloody ants going in and out of the vagina of a woman with her legs spread as an expres-sion of a society that destroys that which has given it life. Some of the interviewees are very aware that symbolic systems tend to legitimize the established order; therefore, they stress the importance of creating new imaginaries. In that sense, some activists are working on their perfor-mances with BDSM representations to, in a pleasant way, visualize power relations and reappropriate the violence that has been denied to women.

> SM is fundamental for us. Power! Bring power in relationships into the open, don't hide it. [...] You can show some things. In our perfo[rmance]s we use them in a very symbolic way. Symbolically. The kings and the queens have a very special relationship. The queens are always dominant, the kings are always submissive, and that's it, full stop. Then, between two queens one can be a submis-sive and the other dominant, that game; but the kings are always submissive. That is what we want to represent. ITU

Drag king workshops are another of the most remarkable practices of the queer feminist collectives (images 2 and 3). They propose transvestism as a political tool, based on the transforming potential of awareness of the performative nature of gender. The dynamic consists of learning to iden-tify macho positions, various forms of aggression and male privileges; but

IMAGES 2 AND 3. Drag king workshop in Vitoria-Gasteiz (Source: 7menos20)

also in experimenting with masculinity as a corporeal experience denied to women. In this way, it is hoped that participants will come to denaturalize masculinity—and femininity—through experiencing gender as a dramatized construction.

Some queer feminist groups are also experimenting with pornographic or pseudo-pornographic workshops, since they reclaim the importance of pornography as a form of sexual learning. They criticize the mainstream pornographic industry, but defend the creation of another type of critical and subversive pornography. Thus, they advocate holding sexual workshops of collective empowerment, in which they experience pornography with their own bodies.

> Pornography creates sex pedagogy, and they deny it to us. It's a lie that pornography is silly. [...] There are things that you think are disgusting and, suddenly, you watch them and get turned on. [...] So, let's not kid ourselves, it's super important. It has to do with sexual hegemonic practices, it has to do with the fact that guys never penetrate each other anally, because that means things, it has to do with us giving blowjobs, with them coming on our faces. [...] The issue is to create critical pornography, to give a critique of that hegemonic pornography, but by doing pornography ... a punk pornography. [...] Do pornography, do it ourselves, put our bodies at stake. That has a tremendous impact. ITU

Queer feminist collectives also conduct other types of dissent, protest, and experimental activities, such as demonstrations and rallies, talks and meetings, art exhibitions, book and documentary launches, and collective readings. According to the information gathered in the interviews, these activities are conducted according to the time available to them and/or the need to respond to different events. But, during the year, there are fixed dates in which they undertake public activity: March 8 (International Women's Day), May 17 (International Day against Homo-Lesbo-Transphobia), June 2 (International Sex Workers' Day), June 28 (International LGBTQI+ Pride Day), November 25 (International Day against Violence against Women) and December 1 (World AIDS Day), to name a few. According to the interviewees, they are responsible for more special days every year.

FEMINIST GAZES, QUEER GAZES

Having mentioned the main discursive and practical characteristics of queer feminist groups in the Basque Country, in this section we will delve into one final aspect: namely, into the axes of tension, the points of affinity and divergence, which exist among different feminist positions. In general, feminist groups with a nonbinary perspective imply change and continuity, at the same time, for the previous feminist collectives or those with a longer trajectory in time, which is sometimes called the "classic feminist movement" by queer feminist groups. On the one hand, they maintain many of their approaches and practices; but, on the other, they have introduced a series of questions, theoretical perspectives, and ways of action that can be considered novel in the Basque feminist panorama.

According to the information obtained in the interviews, feminist collectives with a queer perspective understand feminism as a diverse, broad, and dynamic social movement that seeks to end women's subordination. However, the people interviewed believe that, along with gender inequalities, feminism must address other disparities in our society—such as those of class, ethnicity/race, and sexual orientation, for example—but without it being necessary for all feminist groups to deal with all social inequalities. In short, they argue that each group should opt for a line or axis of work, based on the issues that most motivate the activists. Thus, in particular, queer feminists have opted for the questioning of gender binarism and the critique of heteronormativity, arguing that the feminist struggle and the struggle for sexual liberation must go hand in hand, basically, because they have a common enemy: the heteropatriarchy.

According to the interviews, the introduction of queer approaches has altered the feminist panorama in the Basque Country and made it more complex; so much so, that some people even claim that we are now faced with a "new" feminism, "another type" of feminism. Various terms have been used to refer to it. But most of the people interviewed call it "transfeminism"—understanding it as an internal current within the feminist movement—although there are also those who use other names, such as "post-feminism." However, some activists are very critical of this latter term because of its connotations of surpassing or denying, or even lack of recognition of, previous feminism.

> I am against the "postmodern" concept as something that sur-passes or has left behind Modernity, because there are catego-ries of Modernity that are necessary, just as there are categories of Postmodernity that are necessary as well. Postmodernity must be understood as certain paradigmatic turns [. . .] and full stop. It is not a surpassing, it is not a denial. No. "Post-feminism" has that joke, and we do not like anything. We deny. [. . .] But there is a debate, because there are transfeminists who do want to translate it as "post-feminism." Not me. I don't even want to talk about the subject. ITU

Whatever the case, beyond the debate about the most appropri-ate name for their activism, the interviewees say they move constantly between classic and queer approaches. In some way, they act on these two levels: they question the pillars of our gender system and the way of constructing subjectivities that it brings, criticizing binary and heter-onormative models; but they do not forget that, while they do not like it, it is the gender reality in which we find ourselves. Thus, they work with non-hegemonic ways of experiencing gender, without ignoring at all the inequalities present in normative models. At this point, it is worth noting that, while not considering it somewhat contradictory, some of the inter-viewees do perceive having to move between classic and transfeminist positions as frustrating.

> Now we are most focused on the theme of binarism, on not being in favor of the man/woman binomial gender, that people who do not conform to this scheme should have a place. [. . .] Although lately we have had to turn to classical feminism, because in the

end, it is like the most urgent thing. The same thing that happened forty years ago continues to happen. In other words, it is clear that sexist violence is carried out against women. [. . .] A political struggle to discard the two genders or to broaden the genders would be like a base, as a basic policy; but, in the end, the urgent thing is that women are the ones being killed. LETICIA

According to the information obtained in the interviews, the main political subject in the demands of queer feminist or transfeminist groups are women. As indicated by Leticia's quote, they consider that it is unavoidable that this is so, because of the multiple problems that women face because of the simple fact of being *women*. However, the people interviewed contend that this subject must be expanded, encompassing the diverse experiences of women and, when deemed appropriate, also dealing with other subjects oppressed by our gender system. They also believe that being more relaxed in consideration of who constitutes the feminist subject, leaving the question unanswered, favors the emergence of previously unthought-of political alliances.

Silences are being broken, we are ceasing to see existing realities to speak to us, to see us, and we are also advocating sharing spaces for discussion, theoretical discussion, political discussion, for action. And women, men, queers, dykes, transsexuals are all coinciding in the street . . . and to me that nowadays gives me a lot of satisfaction. [. . .] Machismo will continue to call us to continue working together in the development of strategies that neutralize it more and more until, as they say, like when the fish runs out of water and dies. MIKEL

According to the people interviewed, at first, the irruption of queer feminist groups gave rise to important tensions within the feminist movement. Some activists saw these discourses and actions as attacks or threats, and even accused them of confronting the feminist movement. In this scenario, feminists close to queer approaches felt misunderstood and questioned; yet, even if they had reservations about the classic or earlier feminist movement, considering it something fixed and not radical enough, they never ever stopped identifying themselves as "feminists." Be that as it may, the people interviewed believe that they are things of the past, since they believe that today they have the support and recognition of the feminist movement, that their contributions are valued and that respect predominates. They claim that, at present, the relations between those who have different perspectives are good and that there are hardly any conflicts.

At a discursive level, tensions have mainly revolved around two issues: the treatment of the *women* category; and, linked to the first, the broadening of the political subject of feminism. Transfeminist activists have tried to deconstruct the *women* category. This has meant receiving criticism from some feminists alarmed by the risk of overshadowing the inequalities that women experience, precisely as *women*. However, queer feminists answer that questioning the category does not mean renouncing it. They problematize it, but they continue to use it, because they have not forgotten the specific problems that women suffer. In the same vein, transfeminist groups have been criticized for defending the extension of the political subject of feminism, since that could detract from the strength of women. However, queer feminist activists reject criticism again, claiming, as we have seen, that women are still their main political subject and that, furthermore, it is not true that taking other oppressed subjects into account will harm them.

> That kind of criticism [. . .] I think they have to mature more. Because at first they are not . . . it is not very true that lesbian women are invisible because they talk about transsexuality, it is not very true that trans women are invisible due to the presence of trans men, it is not very true that poofs are made invisible by the presence of lesbian women or trans women or trans men. I think it's a good reflection, because it could be the case that such invisibility actually happened. But, today, that doesn't bother me. MIKEL

At the practical level, the main tensions have derived from the fact that some feminists have experienced transfeminist activists wanting to do something new and different as a lack of political recognition. The people interviewed, however, say they appreciate the activism carried out by the previous feminists or with a longer trajectory, affirming that they are referential for them, although they wish to undertake another type of feminism. Likewise, there have also been tensions over some specific practices of queer feminist groups. The drag king workshops, for example, were very controversial at first, because some feminists considered them anti-feminist and phallocentric, since, from their point of view, they were imitating male models. Pornographic workshops, meanwhile, have also been questioned, because for a large part of the classical feminist movement, pornography is direct violence against women.

Whatever the case, in spite of some divergences, the people interviewed value the fact that the evolution of queer feminism, or transfeminism, has been very positive to date. They believe that it is a current that is in vogue and generates great interest, and that it will remain that way for at least a few years. They emphasize, especially, that it has managed to acknowledge the rut into which the feminist movement had fallen and that it has managed to gain strength and a presence in the streets again, with renewed discourses and practices, and also with a considerable generational change.

Final Point

Queer feminism—transfeminism—is very much alive and active today in the Basque Country. In a short time it has made important contributions to the Basque feminist movement, both discursively and practically. It has been undoubtedly key to rethinking our ideas about gender identity and expression, and about sexual practices and desires. It has provided us with an opportunity to reflect on and work in ways and directions that have not been contemplated before; it has enabled us to imagine new scenarios, experience other experiences. Never free from tensions and divergences, it has had a great diffusion and a wide acceptance within Basque feminist collectives. However, its history is still to be written, since it is yet to be seen what its long-term impact will be.

Bibliography

Aliaga, Juan Vicente. "Pujanza (y miseria) de un nombre. Sobre la teoría *queer* y su plasmación en el activismo y el arte contemporáneo." In *Transgenéric@s,* edited by Juan Vicente Aliaga, Lawrence Rinder, Nayland Blake, and Mar Villaespesa, 9-33. Donostia-San Sebastián: Gipuzkoako Foru Aldundia/Diputación Foral de Gipuzkoa, 1998.

Barker, Meg-John. *Queer. A Graphic History.* Illustrated by Jules Scheele. London: Icon Books Ltd, 2016.

Benhabib, Seyla. "Feminismo y posmodernidad: una difícil alianza." In *Teoría feminista: de la Ilustración a la globalización. Del feminismo liberal a la posmodernidad,* edited by Celia Amorós Puente and Ana de Miguel Álvarez, 319-342. Madrid: Minerva Ediciones, 2005.

Butler, Judith. *Gender Trouble: Feminism and the Subversion of Identity.* New York: Routledge, 1990.

De Lauretis, Teresa. "Queer Theory. Lesbian and Gay Sexualities." *Differences: A Journal of Feminist Cultural Studies* 3, no. 2 (1990): 3-18.

Epelde Pagola, Edurne, Miren Aranguren Etxarte, and Iratxe Retolaza Gutierrez. *Gure genealogia feministak. Euskal Herriko Mugimendu Feministaren Kronika bat.* Andoain: Emagin, 2015.

Esteban, Mari Luz. "Identidades de género, feminismo, sexualidad y amor: Los cuerpos como agentes." *Política y sociedad* 46, no. 1-2 (2009): 27-41.

Fernández, Sandra, and Aitzole Araneta. "Genealogías trans(feministas)." In *Transfeminismos. Epistemes, fricciones y flujos,* edited by Miriam Solá and Elena Urko, 45-58. Tafalla: Txalaparta, 2013.

Medeak. "Violencia y transfeminismo. Una mirada situada." In *Transfeminismos. Epistemes, fricciones y flujos,* edited by Miriam Solá and Elena Urko, 73-79. Tafalla: Txalaparta, 2013.

PutaBolloNegraTransFeminista Sarea. "Manifestu TransFeminista." In *Genero-ariketak. Feminismoaren subjektuak,* edited by Isa Castillo and Iratxe Retolaza, 73-74. Donostia-San Sebastián: edo!, 2013.

Romero, Carmen, Silvia García, and Carlos Bargueiras. "Introducción . . . El eje del mal es heterosexual." In *El eje del mal es heterosexual: figuraciones, movimientos y prácticas feministas queer,* edited by Carlos Bargueiras, Carmen Romero, and Silvia García, 17-27. Madrid: Traficantes de Sueños, 2005.

Sáez, Javier. "El contexto sociopolítico de surgimiento de la teoría queer. De la crisis del Sida a Foucault." In *Teoría queer. Políticas bolleras, maricas, trans, mestizas,* edited by David Córdoba, Javier Sáez, and Paco Vidarte, 67-76. Madrid: Egales, 2005.

Stevenson, Angus, and Maurice Waite, eds. *Concise Oxford English Dictionary* (twelfth edition). Oxford: Oxford University Press, 2011.

Trujillo, Gracia. "Identidades, estrategias, resistencias." Coordinadora Feminista. Accessed February 28, 2010. http://www.feministas.org/identidades-estrategias.html.

NOTES

1 This text is based on a research project entitled *Discursos y prácticas queer en los movimientos feministas vascos* (Queer discourses and practices in the Basque feminist movements), a dissertation required for a master's degree in feminist and gender studies at the University of the Basque Country (UPV/EHU) in the academic year 2009/2010. The ethnographic material dates from 2010.

2 "Transfeminism" can be understood as a queer feminism. As will be explained in more detail throughout the text, Basque feminist groups with nonbinary and contrary approaches to heteronormativity do not often use the word "queer," considering it a little-known Anglicism in their context. They prefer to define themselves with other kinds of names.

3 I am referring to groups such as LSD (Lesbianas Sin Duda or Lesbianas Sexo Delicioso, among other possibilities) and the Radical Gai, both influenced by queer movements in the United States, England, and France.

4 Epelde. *Gure genealogia feministak. Euskal Herriko Mugimendu Feministaren Kronika bat,* 429.

5 Epelde, *Gure genealogia feministak,* 496-497.

6 Fernández. "Genealogías trans(feministas)," 52-53.

7 PutaBolloNegraTransFeminista Sarea, "Manifestu TransFeminista," in *Genero-ariketak. Feminismoaren subjektuak,* ed. Isa Castillo and Iratxe Retolaza (Donostia-San Sebastián: edo!, 2013), 73.

8 Medeak. "Violencia y transfeminismo. Una mirada situada," 73.

9 Sáez, "El contexto sociopolítico de surgimiento de la teoría queer. De la crisis del Sida a Foucault," 67-72.

10 Romero. "Introducción . . . El eje del mal es heterosexual," 24.

11 Stevenson. *Concise Oxford English Dictionary* (twelfth edition), 1177.

12 Aliaga. "Pujanza (y miseria) de un nombre," 15-16.

13 Aliaga. "Pujanza (y miseria) de un nombre," 9.

14 AZT is a retroviral medication, created in the 1960s as a cancer drug, but abandoned in the '70s because of its high level of toxicity and its strong side effects. In 1987, however, its use was again approved to try to combat AIDS.

15 Trujillo. "Identidades, estrategias, resistencias."

16 Esteban. "Identidades de género, feminismo, sexualidad y amor: Los cuerpos como agentes," 36.

17 Teresa de Lauretis, "Queer Theory. Lesbian and Gay Sexualities," *Differences: A Journal of Feminist Cultural Studies* 3, no. 2 (1990), 3-18.

18 Butler, *Gender Trouble: Feminism and the Subversion of Identity.*

19 Trujillo, "Identidades, estrategias, resistencias."

20 Barker, *Queer. A Graphic History,* 62.

21 Benhabib, "Feminismo y posmodernidad: una difícil alianza," 322-323.

22 Member of 7menos 20, a collective of feminist lesbians, self-titled "lesbotransfeminist," created in 2006.

23 Dyke.

24 Poof.

25 Activist in the radical feminist and transfeminist group Medeak, formed in 2000.

26 Activist in Garaipen, a feminist group made up of migrant and Basque women, created in 2002.

27 Member of EHGAM, a sexual liberation gay-lesbian collective formed in 1977.

28 For several years, the coordinator was made up of EHGAM, Euskal Herriko Bilgune Feminista, Garaipen and Medeak. However, in recent years there have been attempts to integrate more groups and individuals.

4

Fast, Slow, and Still Waters: An Overview of LGBTQI+* Politics in the Southern Basque Country

Jokin Azpiazu Carballo
University of the Basque Country, EHU

> The last task I'd set for myself was finding the Stonewall
> bar. I remembered the impact when we heard about the
> battle with the cops in 1969. I wanted to ask a passerby to
> take a picture in front of it. I thought someday, after I'd
> died, someone might find the photo and understand me
> a little better.
> —"Do you know where the Stonewall bar is?" I asked
> two gay men who were leaning up against a lamppost in
> Sheridan Square.
> —"That used to be the bar." One of the men pointed to a
> bagel shop.
>
> —*Leslie Feinberg,* Stone Butch Blues *(Ann
> Arbor, MI: Firebrand Books, 1993), 263-64.*

INTRODUCTION AND EXPLANATIONS OF THE METHODOLOGY

The aim of this chapter is to conduct an overview of LGBTQI+*[1] politics in the contemporary Southern Basque Country (SBC). To the extent
that everything expressed here is part of a wider research project, it makes
sense to speak of an overview. The aim of the chapter is not to offer a specific cartography, but rather to identify several issues within the movement around sexual freedom through interviews with numerous activists
and collectives and to suggest ideas to delve more deeply into the main
lines of debate.

This research is part of another and wider research development space, specifically that termed "LGBT subjectivities in popular

movements in the Basque Country," within which I am completing my dissertation. The study of LGBTQI+* politics is one of four pillars of that dissertation. The dissertation is based on the experience of people who identify themselves as gay, lesbian, or trans* (in the widest sense) but who are active in some other movements. That section is based on sixteen personal interviews with activists in labor union, ecologist, or feminist movements. This chapter, in turn, is based on eleven deep interviews, often in groups, with activists and collectives active today. In two cases, those activists were not by then active in the movements and therefore they offered a more historical perspective. In one case, the interview was conducted with one individual activist who is a major point of reference in the subject even though not a member of a formally organized collective. The groups have used different forms and terms to define themselves and their politics. Although they have different levels of relationships with the political institutions (city councils, provincial councils, the Basque government, and so on), in most cases they were independently organized groups that did not receive direct subsidies. The targets of this research were not really groups that work in the institutional area (that would be another research project), although many of those are active and also take part in public mobilizations.

To conclude, the selection of the groups did not aim to be a stratified sample, even though some diversity was guaranteed from the perspective of the composition of the groups. With regard to the quantity, one could say that just as many or more groups and initiatives were not included. I repeat: the goal was not to assemble a specific cartography or a map of contemporary movements, but rather to consider the problems, lines of inquiry, and debates. To facilitate that, the fragments of interviews that will be used throughout the chapter will not be identified with specific groups or their characteristics. Moreover, in the cases of group interviews, I did not want to give in to distinguishing among the opinions of different people, within the groups, and, in many cases, to the richer opinions and contradictions also within the expressions of the same subject. I believe that LGBTQI+* politics is experiencing a moment of redefining itself and thinking together, and this chapter seeks to encourage those debates.

With regard to the research methodology, Adele E. Clarke's *Situational Analysis* (Clarke 2005) is the starting point for my argument. Clarke's and Kathy Charmaz's (Charmaz 2006) *Grounded Theory* argument are based on the foundations of the methodology, without overlooking the useful aspects of this theory, incorporating an updated epistemological feminist and post-structuralist perspective. Following this argument, the research interviews were the first task. After codifying and analyzing them with maps and developing different angles, several theoretical elements were added to the analysis. It was, therefore, an inductive process. The main reasons for this were certain features of this specific study. Because scant research has been conducted on LGBTQI+ topics in the Basque Country, it seemed more interesting to me to start with the ideas of those taking part, instead of applying the theories created in other geopolitical and cultural contexts to our case. As Egaña Etxeberria suggests:

> The queer theory and movement came (. . .) from the English-speaking world and above all the USA (. . .) nor is "importing" such ideas a problem-free task. I would say that when we ourselves have received contributions to queer theories or carried out studies of queer literature, sometimes we have followed blindly theories from the USA (. . .) that nor have we looked sufficiently, for example, at our own agendas that have been developed around sexual freedom or the relations in recent decades among sexual-freedom and other similar movements in the Basque Country itself (Egaña Etxeberria 2017, 70).

In any event, the study does not ignore the contributions of theories on sexuality, gender identity, and movements. Instead of understanding the inductive process as epistemological certainty, I have taken it to be a strategic and experimental option, acknowledging that it opens up some doors just as it closes others.

That does not mean that the methodology is restricted to that focus. Some elements of participatory research have also been taken into account (McIntyre 2008), for example, by defining the research objectives through the help of a group comprised of activists and researchers or organizing contrast sessions. At the same time, following the arguments of narrative productions (Montenegro and Balasch 2003), transcriptions of the interviews were returned to the participants and they were given the option to make changes, although this has not led to any more profound development of the narrative production, mainly because of the limitations of time and resources.

THE FAST WATERS OF LGBTQI+* POLITICS: NORMALIZATION AND PINK CAPITALISM
Contemporary activists explain clearly the profound influence of transformations that have been experienced in recent years. They know very well,
however, that the rhythms of those changes around them and, as a consequence, in their activity are at different speeds. Movements, then, must
negotiate continuously the stages between fast-flowing and still waters, to
a large extent in recent decades at the state level, but also in the Southern
Basque Country (SBC), as a result of the changes and events that have
taken place. In his 2007 work *Ética marica,* Paco Vidarte anticipated the
suspicion surrounding LGBTQI+ groups following the Zapatero government's recognition of same-sex marriages: "If from below we do not trans-
mit to them what we want, what we need, they are going to become mere
managers, they will run out of ideas, they will turn to care work" (Vidarte
2007, 76). Those interviewed had many different opinions about that, but
they agreed on highlighting one point of inflection, for good or bad:

> And from then on, well, I think the movement . . . the movement
> did not fully understand how to define a new agenda and popu-
> larize that new agenda. After so much time saying "we want to
> get married, we want to get married, if we get married, an eternal
> spring will happen" . . . and well, you can get married now and so
> what? [INT11]

From that moment on, it looks like everything has been moving
swiftly in the political and social scene opening up, and as soon as the
groups get to name what is happening around them, it changes again. The
most prominent phenomena, those that activists are most critical of, are
the development of pink capitalism, by means of homologating the normalization of LGBTQI+ identities (especially of gay men), and the place
that liberal politics has sought in LGBTQI+ subjects.

In recent years, as in several northern hemisphere countries, economic
activities linked to LGBTQI+ identities have multiplied. In the same
way that identities outside those of heterosexuality and cis norms have
found a spotlight and place in our societies, the strategy of contemporary
capitalism has been to establish, stereotype, perpetuate, and link those
identities to consumption. Products are beginning to be created aimed
at L-G-B-T people, specifically linked to the service and leisure sectors,
but not just there. Several mechanisms linked to reproduction and family
life remain in the hands of private companies. The interviewees link this

process to the image of an economically successful, local, cis, gay man that has become the reference point. Even though pink capitalism, or as some participants term it, gaypitalism, may vary, they recognize it especially affects men. From the perspective of a gender critique, most lesbian and trans* people, especially women, have been expelled from the center stage of this process. To cite one example, in hotels aimed at gay people that will open in Donostia and Bilbao, the restrooms are distinguished according to gender, without taking into account the demands of trans* people.

Many groups are more intent than ever on being anti-capitalist. All of the groups interviewed revealed a critical view of the economic system, if not direct confrontation. In the same way that capitalism uses LGBTQI+ identities for its own benefit, LGBTQI+* politics point out that that there are also spaces of resistance to that, by means of politics along the lines of "not in our name."

Many activists see capitalism as a machine for creating identities and this explains the explosion of sexual identities at that level. The market increasingly atomizes and breaks down identities, transmitting the promise of uniqueness to those identities through products and personalized messages, while at the same time people have the sensation of getting lost in an infinite anonymity. This individualistic paradox (Esposito 2012), with regard to the experiences linked to sexuality and gender, can transform liberating forces into coercion. Hence, it is imperative to take into account the influence of the liberal perspective. When LGBTQI+* politics are based purely on individual rights, those identities are transformed into the pure logic of the market (Espinosa Miñoso 1999).

Many people also connect the state of contemporary movements with the liberal perspective. One could say that liberalism and agendas based on rights (chiefly that of marriage, the right to adopt, that of receiving gender-affirming treatment in the public health system, and changing official documents according to the lived gender)[2] have left the movements "little to demand." On the contrary, the participants believe that a movement that embraces a critique of capitalism, racism, and liberalism has a major task ahead of it: "*From the perspective of neoliberalism there's nothing to do, since we've achieved our rights and so on, but from a radical point of view there's still plenty of work to do to get the roots of it and smash the system. For us, there's a huge amount of work to do ahead*" [INT03].

But the reason for questioning capitalism and liberalism is not just solidarity. As noted above, the activists feel responsible for what can be done in their name. At this level, to critique normalization processes is a tool for questioning wider phenomena. For example, those who criticize having placed the right to get married front and center in LGBTQI+* politics, introduce different debates. First, that achievement reveals the homologation of the needs and customs of heterosexual society, instead of exploring different models of coexistence by making homosexual practice acceptable everywhere. Second, that critique raises the issue of that demand as reflective of the interests of certain specific subjects carried out on behalf of a whole community. Those were locals and therefore had the right to get married, and those that organize their relationships in established couples.

Same-sex marriage has not just been expressed as an achievement or a victory. In the global geopolitical panorama, it has been interpreted as an expression of the treatment given by societies to sexual diverse societies, with those that recognize same-sex marriage understood as progressive and those that do not as reactionary. Often one only need look at the "global LGBT rights map" used to reveal the contradictions of this. In that ranking of rights, many of the countries in the top positions are not the most conducive to living in for LGBTQI+ people, or not at least for most LGBTQI+ people. Many of them are countries with serious economic imbalances, very high levels of violence against LGBTQI+ people and women, or unacceptable unemployment levels in the case of trans* women. Some of them are the world's major arms producers, or have been condemned at the international level on numerous occasions for infringing human rights both within and outside their borders, such as in the case of Israel. This raises two issues: one, that marriage is not a privileged expression of the conditions experienced by LGBTQI+ people, as many people suggest; and two, that LGBTQI+ rights are often used from a geopolitical perspective to hide the harmful policies of states and point out certain other states as crooked (Puar 2017). In that sense, critiquing normalization and the institutionalization of rights is no mere rhetorical maneuver, but also a denouncement of the devious uses that can be made of LGBTQI+* politics.

Linked to institutionalization, the two sides of those processes are revealed in the study. Most are linked, like Vidarte does above, to aid. From a historical perspective, SBC movements have given great importance to aid, especially in the first decade after the transition (López Romo 2008), as did women's movements (Zabala González 2008). Initially, that aid was organized through mutual support groups but in time a professional approach came to dominate in many places, for two main reasons: to begin with, the people who approached the groups were not always seeking political activism but rather protection and support. Thereafter, giving such support became the chief activity of some groups. Groups that were founded purely by activists also saw that they were limited when it came to resources and skills, without knowing how to cope with certain situations. At that level professionalization brought benefits from a service perspective. But one of the effects that amateur aid and activists could offer, namely, that those who went in search of aid subsequently became activists, was weakened.

That process brought increasingly closer ties with the institutions, because most of the policies and interventions conducted in the fields of aid and, later, education are done via financial aid on the part of public institutions. In that process the groups have created a variety of relationships with the institutions: some do not want to know anything about them, others have specific interactions at certain times via organizing particular activities or certain grants, and still others maintain permanent relationships. Those close-distant positions create specific problems for the groups. Many cited, for example, that the institutions use the groups to legitimize their policies instead of including activist groups from the beginning in designing those.

To conclude, many mentioned that these elements have placed LGBTQI+* politics in a difficult situation, especially in the face of popular movements that defend orthodox left wing positions. Being absorbed by capitalism and the institutions, or revealing a clearly liberal political identity, is an accusation that the movements must hear often. The following transfeminist activist summarizes that exercise of recuperation or reterritorialization (Deleuze and Guattari 2002), underscoring that it is not exclusive to the feminist movement or LGBTQI+* politics:

> The critique of the relationship feminism has with capitalism comes from a very male left-wing stance, and it bothers me. Well, capitalism tries to commercialize and appropriate and break the potential of all movements. Now that feminism is on the rise, it will be feminism it appropriates, but it doesn't mean this is exclusive of feminism . . . [INT10]

Nowadays, the movements are agents in a whirlpool of fast-flowing water made up of all that economic, geopolitical, and cultural transformation. Continually developed and complex analyses are being conducted on this. Yet at the same time, they are moved by a completely different rhythm in still waters. It has had the general effect on them of weakening activism and political commitment (most of the groups are very small), and they are clear that finding an effective subject for activism is a slow and delicate process.

Still Waters: Experiences, Identities, and Subjectivity Politics

The notion of experience is central to the theories of new popular movements. As Maria Livia Alga summarizes very well, theoreticians have given much importance to that element in post-1960s movements: each of the individuals making up the movements, those who differentiate themselves from others and create opposition strategies, has a consciousness of sharing the experience itself (Livia Alga 2018, 140-143). Verta Taylor and Nancy E. Whittier, however, claim that those elements linked to identity are responsible for "new" social movements and have always been present in all movements, including workers' movements as well (Taylor and Whittier 1992). Richard Day accuses that category of new social movements of being a sociological image, saying that it is an abstraction. Furthermore, in underscoring the link they have with personal experience, he contends that we have taken those movements, and only those, to be cultural or symbolic movements, without considering the different spheres of influence they have (Day 2016, 105).

Whether a tendency of some or all movements, a consciousness of common experiences in mobilization processes develops, and there is a pronounced tendency to strengthen identities. At this level there is open and lively debate now within LGBTQI+* politics. Undoubtedly, LGBTQI+* politics are part of restructuring processes in all politics, just as in the feminist movement and others (Esteban 2015). Those processes take the political out of the exclusively rational space toward a more complex space, considering the emotional sphere as also political. Activists demand that personal experiences must have a place in that sense, but most also recall the excesses that can emerge in this regard. The risk is not bringing our personal experiences or elements that cause harm in life front and center, but rather the ways in which they are politicized. A collective exercise must be done to politicize them, and, thus, these experiences become political by placing them within a broader structure. But, given the centrality that contemporary liberal capitalism gives personal experience, that experience can be fossilized and a stable identity can be created, one that can be hard to articulate at the political level because of its atomic nature.

> For me, there is no substance to that. That's something that under-pins your experience and not a categorization based on the system. That is, for me, identity politics, a term and some positions that are based on pure experience (. . .) For us, identities are created out of oppressions, and not the other way round. [INT03]

In these groups' interpretations, oppression systems can create identi-ties. But one must tread with caution when theorizing whole oppression systems out of personal experiences because one loses sight of the system. Those are very delicate considerations. The theoretical tools we have to understand the structures are not monolithic, and therefore some experi-ences have been central to add several forms of oppression to them. Let us consider, for example, women's oppression. At which moment and when theorizing about whose experience was it understood as structural? At this level, the movements confront the constant fragmentation of iden-tities. Establishing those identities can avoid political articulation, but considering them "not political" can close doors on some questionings.

This atomization of identities is very clearly visible in the case of digi-tal networks, a privileged space for activism during the last decade. Some activists sense that such endless identity production takes place in the net-works and consider the dynamics that unfold there (for example, restrict-ing political debate in networks such as Twitter to a rhetorical struggle) to be harmful: there is no mechanism in the networks for enriching debates that may be activated in other spaces of popular movements, and, con-sequently, they just receive the collateral damage of hot-tempered argu-ments. Identity clashes are often at the root of those arguments, and calls for individuality are encouraged, distorting the feminist maxim that the personal is political:

> About social media, one of my concerns is how we are falling over and over again into super hedonistic agendas. What's going on are stories in the first person by people talking about their things and since "the personal is political." I tell you my story and that's all . . . That's ok, but, well, for the personal to be political you must politicize it . . . [INT04]

In those processes, the place of experience is, then, problematic. If we create a closed identity out of each experience, we cannot articulate an effective political subject. But several activists remind us that, in the name of effective political subjects, on many occasions, experience has been overlooked. Many activists have doubts about what to do with the pain being gay, lesbian, or trans* has created. Some see activism as an option to make a different kind of use of "those dark feelings," to use anger in a political way. That pain that may lay behind activism, which cuts through experience, is an indispensable element to confront clashes between identities and positions. When it comes to implementing a campaign, which words to use, who will represent us, with which groups to make alliances . . . All of this has a clear political dimension and, as mentioned above, politics cannot be linked to strategy and rationality alone. That pain, and that enduring pain, operating from a position of endless pain, marks these debates deeply. But to avoid such melancholic politics, the pain must be brought front and center, not to function out of the pain but to be able to continue working alongside such pain (Braidotti 2018, 172).

Using identity as a starting point can be appropriate to undertake such work and to become a political subject that way. It is a starting point but not the objective (Rich 1984), because, specifically, any politics that takes as its goal strengthening identities, brings with it the foreclosure of those identities and the rigid protection of their boundaries, and in most cases it is a source of exclusions (Gamson 1997). This activist, for example, defends that notion of "fag" as a political subject, within the broader struggle of transfeminism:

> I think it's interesting to be a fag subject as a starting point, a start-
> ing point toward somewhere else. My voice, my experience, my
> participation comes from here (. . .) [I need] a more closed cate-
> gory, than transfeminist, a category that makes you feel more com-
> fortable in order to create smaller structures (. . .) In that sense it's
> interesting. But I have no idea where it may lead me in my struggle
> at the end . . . But as a starting point, I like it. [INT09]

That specific starting point has not been the only such beginning position demanded. The movements name different political subjects. Some of them see no problem in considering specific identities as subjects, at the same time they question identities created by the powers. As such, they favor transforming the recovery of old names (fag, dyke) or creating new unified subjects out of that (*transmaricabibollo*, or transfagdyke).³ Others suggest strengthening the LGBTQI+ collective subject, or the name gay as an all-embracing term for all L-G-B-T-Q-I+ people. There are also those who do not connect their activity with the LGBTQI+ movement, even though they emphasize that they are in touch on LGBTQI+* politics. They proclaim their support for feminist lesbianism as a political position, or incorporate transfeminism.

Each subject can have its potentialities, from the perspective of the contemporary SBC. A critique of the gay subject as white, male, and economically powerful has been raised. Fag politics places gender subversion front and center, making use of a feminist perspective that has not always been present historically in the gay movement. In the event of articulating this well, respecting the specific spaces and references of feminism, the activists believe that it opens up the possibility of new alliances, calling into question the transformative potential of homosexuality: "That's why the whole fag thing is important, because homosexuality is no longer a warhorse. [From power instances] they are taking the whole fag thing away from us and replacing it with homosexuality." [INT01] This activist wants to reclaim back a piece of homosexuality that has been historically removed in order to create a respectable gay subject: one that is very campy, sassy, not beautiful, and effeminate.

Lesbianism is also a specific subject that offers major potentialities. If the fag subject struggled against its restriction, the lesbian subject struggles against its erasure, again to break the neutralization of its political potential. From a feminist interpretation, lesbianism is not just one's internal desire, a desire that should be placed alongside other desires, and granted respect. From a reading of compulsory heterosexuality (Rich 1980), lesbianism can be a practice that helps to erase the circuits of heterosexuality and, as a consequence, it is not just an internal feeling expressed externally but a political position that develops by means of dismantling desire for men. Sara Ahmed, for example, posits lesbianism *as an orientation*, like a job that must be done, in the same way as heterosexuality as well (Ahmed 2019). From this perspective these activists are clear: "Our activism is aimed at dykes in our circles or at possible future dykes (. . .) In the end we create possibilities of being." [INT08] Their activism is not just a call for respect. It is essential to talk about it as a transformative perspective. Even if others interpret their argument as essentialist they do not seek to fix a lesbian identity, because they understand it as an open and nomadic entity (Braidotti 2000). Their argument is based not on what there is but what may be created and in that sense it projects toward the future.

Others have suggested (re-)creating a unified LGBTQI+ subject, and this also has, of course, its potentialities. Historically, what has been understood as the LGBTQI+ subject has been a space of marginalization and exclusion. Often, all of those who were not cissexual gay men were relegated to a secondary level. Lesbians and the trans* communities, for example, have had more conflictive relations within the movement (Stryker 2017), but that does not mean that that subject cannot be renewed from a radical perspective. To do that, listening exercises are essential, especially to lead through the reality of trans* women who have been relegated to the small print. That reformulation takes the spirit of the early movement as its chief reference point, in which the word "gay" was used as an umbrella term to denote very diverse realities (Duberman 2018). In the SBC, too, from the start that was the terminology used when speaking about the "gay liberation movement." But the creation of lesbian groups, almost from the very beginning, also explains that the unified term gay masked exclusions, those that even resulted in a split in Bizkaia.[4] Whatever the case, the argument raises the idea of a shared space, and confronting the atomizing dynamic of liberalism by means of a broader subject. The proposal to create transfagdyke spaces follows the same pattern, even though those in favor of LGBTQI+ spaces have pointed out the limits on the capacities of the movements to reclaim those words, defending, instead, a more inclusive LGBTQI+ term:

> "We don't use transfagdyke, because there are a lot of people who identify with that but within LGBT communities there are also a lot of people that will not identify with that. Embracing insults as empowerment is totally valid, but just in a personal way (. . .) We know that a lot of people who identify with that and we must acknowledge this, but at the same time we must also acknowledge the power of what words mean or the power they have." [INT03]

LGBTQI+* politics can suggest more subjects, specific or unified, than the interviewees raised during the research. In many cases, however, and beyond the nature of a proposal, activists have underscored the need to create alliances, speaking from intersectional perspectives. A plethora of surnames are added to those political subjects either implicitly or

explicitly (anticapitalist, antiracist . . .). How we approach those articulation spaces, however, is not yet clear. Will those different political subjectivities trust in the power they have to take in others? Or will we approach
other spaces with those particular subjects (be it a fag, lesbian, TMBB,
or LGBTQI+ subject)? And when we approach, what will those spaces
define? The movements are at a crossroads. On the one hand, they still
take those subjective edifices as necessary: (trans)feminist, LGBTQI+,
queer, TMBB, feminist lesbian . . . On the other, an empty space is necessary for profound and effective alliances (Livia Alga 2018), one that
gives movements major vertigo, specifically because of the fear we have
of losing our specificity.

Beyond that, another dilemma opens up: if the politics carried out based
on purely LGBTQI+ matters and fixed identities (that is, without taking
into account class, backgrounds, and aptitudes) do not satisfy the groups,
does it still make sense to defend these LGTB subjectivities? Or, looked
at from the other side, does the subject have any special predisposition or
potentiality from being LGBTQI+ to understand and fight against other
kinds of oppression?

Ahmed uses a revision of some phenomenological contributions to go
more deeply into the orientation concept from a queer perspective, and to
explore nonnormative sexuality, especially lesbianism, from that gaze. She
presents heterosexuality as an orientation, and she pays special attention
to the tangle and disorientation created by being diverted from that orientation. In her opinion, that disorientation has the potential to facilitate
different, oblique gazes. That does not imply an apology for disorientation
(Ahmed 2019: 218), but she suggests that we explore its potential. On the
same level some activists see that open possibility within nonnormative
sexuality and gender identities, even though they do not want to idealize
them. In the words of this fag activist, for example:

> "The fag is also going to be a lot more sensitive when it comes to
> defending all postures, much more than the gay . . . [5] The fag is
> going to defend the posture of the gay and the fag, and the gay is
> going to defend just his, but not that of the fag, and even less if
> they are poor, because he ignores them (. . .)" [INT06]

Placing experience, identity, and political subjects together is a difficult task for movements that currently operate within LGBTQI+* politics. On the one hand, experiences are essential to demand those positions

and, as we will see later, to construct a precise and broad demand. On the other, undertaking an individual and non-constitutive interpretation of those experiences opens up the possibilities of falling into processes of being absorbed by the market. In those processes identities can become fixed, closed, and exclusionary and, at the same time, a useful control discipline for powers and institutions. If that were not enough, constructing political subjects calls for some minimum identifications, and those identifications, in the LGBTQI+* case too, do not happen just out of the references created by movements. To avoid becoming a sectorial struggle, movements must think about how to articulate with other subjects and groups, thinking about how to articulate internal and external boundaries and empty spaces. Yet, is it essential for them to just think about this and nothing else, or could doing something be the key?

EXHAUSTED WATERS? PROPOSALS, AGENDAS, AND STRATEGIES FOR LGBTQI+* POLITICS

In the following text, I will briefly cite some of the problems surrounding agendas, proposals, and strategies on the agenda of LGBTQI+* politics in SBC. I have linked this section to exhausted waters, because of the kind of connection to all the meanings that word has. First, it expresses an act of being very tired or losing strength. Second, it can also be a reference to something that is materially or symbolically ending or running out. Third, it reflects the weariness resulting from something that happens or is repeated a lot. At different levels the movements express the weariness resulting from confrontation and notes the expiration of agendas that articulated specific proposals in an easy way. Many feel a sensation of repeating profound structural topics over and over again, with little response.

Reinventions are customary in situations of exhaustion. Following long silences for some years, LGBTQI+* politics are being reinvented. Many activists are finding renewed strength in the aforementioned new and renewed forms of subjectivity. The agendas and strategies of LGBTQI+* politics must be updated, and it is essential to leave the past behind. The initial task is to create new agendas, but to begin, many activists question the idea of an agenda itself. We say that movements must have a clear agenda in the same way as they must articulate specific demands and direct them to the institutions. Yet that is not the aim of all movements (Day 2016). Having a very specific and supposedly achievable character, the most socially prominent agendas (marriage, adoption ...) were not so helpful in their day in projecting their voices in broader circles, and it does not help those who currently do not want to pursue their demands from legal or administrative perspectives:

> When is a discourse created, and when do you consider a demand has been met? When they are institutionalized? (. . .) Whether there is a law ... I don't care if there's a marriage law. Of course this is great, but in my everyday life, as it is ... I understand that it's much more about the day-to-day and in the networks we get to weave in the public arena, right there. [INT08]

Calling into question the notion of an agenda itself is, one way or another, the response in advance to the accusation from some other movements and institutions. In the opinion of some, the groups' agendas are restricted to the symbolic field, and they claim that activists operate in more than just that field. Moreover, they also emphasize the importance of incorporating new elements and transforming the social imaginary, understanding this as political work. For example, consider the emphasis on discourses that can place heterosexuality as a system rather than a sexual practice. Nevertheless, I have perceived difficulties to connect the symbolic field or what Fraser terms those politics of recognition (Fraser 2010) and other fields in specific tasks on the agenda. While they acknowledge criticism of the concept itself, some actvitists also feel the need to specify the agenda and believe that the movements have had difficulties in doing this in recent years. They underscore the need to perform specific diagnoses at that level to better understand the consequences that the everyday lack of recognition may bring, for example, at a socioeconomic level.

At that level it is difficult for some groups to raise their demands in some areas because of the relationship they have with an institution. For example, it is very difficult to make suggestions regarding the economy if we do not have the state as an interlocutor in our politics. One of the few proposals I have come across, from an economic and autonomous perspective, was an exchange network among lesbians using online forums that encourage cooperation in everyday economic matters with the aim of strengthening communities. In most other cases, noninstitutional groups have not proposed specific measures to examine work or employment. In the matter of agendas, then, these two elements must be taken into account. On the one hand, at moments when intervention politics are being recharacterized, it is essential, too, to transform the ways of conducting politics and, as a result, the demands. On the other, when it comes to creating new agendas, our strategies present opportunities and limits, and we may have difficulties to connect different aspects of social life (economy, politics, symbolic recognition . . .)

Dean Spade suggests a model to study group activity, specifically after examining critically the validity of legal and administrative strategies. From the proposals of the Miami Workers Center group, he takes the *Four Pillars of Social Justice Infrastructure* model: policy, consciousness, service, and power (Spade 2015: 184-185). The first promotes institutional and administrative change, while the second strives to transform social paradigms. The third seeks to offer help to those experiencing maltreatment as the result of oppression, and the goal of the last is to encourage popular power. Even though the model is linked closely to political forms in the United States, it would be worth asking whether in our case, LGBTQI+* politics are employing those pillars.

Few demands exist in the first pillar now, with the exception of those still reclaimed by the trans* collective with regard to health and documentation. Likewise, demands are aimed at specific institutions, for example, at universities. The work of most of the groups interviewed is clearly in the second and third pillars. They want to transform the image of society by different actions and initiatives, I would say, taking as a primary interlocutor groups and individuals that have a minimum consciousness about the topic: they seek to promote understanding about sexuality and gender matters together with other kinds of oppression. At the same time, importance is given to the empowerment of LGBTQI+ subjects, creating community strength and maintaining self-empowerment with regard to institutions. The idea of service seems weak, specifically in groups that do not have stable relationships with institutions. Although they are capable of affecting people's daily lives, those politics are not structured. For the most part they remain in the hands of the institutions, which make no connections between the third and fourth pillars. Offering aid to people on a day-to-day basis does not mean that collective empowerment processes take place, nor bottom-up organizational self-empowerment.

One would wonder whether it is desirable for all the groups in LGBTQI+* politics to work those four pillars or whether it is possible to understand these politics as a multiple- formed monster with many heads.

The first option would complicate the work of many groups and probably make it more difficult for them to endure. The second puts us at risk of losing the connection among the different pillars. The choice, then, is strategic.

With regard to strategies, groups fluctuate between intimacy and distance. On the one hand, initiatives want to be self-support spaces, with two objectives therein: they want to give support to members who do not have it in some other areas and transform those spaces into ones of radical experimentation. They want to be affirmative alternatives at that level (Braidotti 2018, 169). In actively looking outward, on the contrary, it is hard for them, as noted, to reach certain areas. On many levels, as some major mobilizations demonstrate, distance is created between the groups and the communities they supposedly represent. I say "supposedly," because many groups do not seek to represent anyone and regard as essential limiting their politics to the local space: *"More than final objectives, we are interested in particular actions that have their effect . . . we focus on local actions because we want very specific things."* [INT01]

In many cases, then, groups appear like useful mechanisms or protocols, yet the scalability of that initiative remains to be studied (Hester 2018). In any event, activists also give great importance to the element of group relations, and to creating coalitions, to protecting what Helen Hester herself terms the *mesopolitical* space, one that, it goes without saying, is conflictive in most cases.

Short Conclusions and Some Views

Within our geographical area, studying LGBTQI+* politics is a complex task. We often introduce the theoretical and analytical apparatuses of the sociology of social movements and make an effort to fit the work of collectives and groups in those devices. Frequently, the tools stemming from the theorizing efforts of the movements themselves offer more help, especially if we want to assist those movements with our analyses. It is also essential to adapt those tools to local realities if we want to take into account geopolitical and cultural particularities. In writing this chapter, for example, the short report published by the Joxemi Zumalabe Foundation, titled "Gatazkak, borroka moldeak eta kultura politikoa herri mugimenduetan" (Conflicts, forms of struggle, and political culture in popular movements) (Joxemi Zumalabe Fundazioa 2019), can offer some appropriate clues when it comes to thinking critically about discussing LGBTQI+* politics. I will leave that for another occasion.

LGBTQI+* politics are in a moment of restructuring in the Southern Basque Country. Within the need to respond to the changes in the general panorama, the necessity has emerged for a rethink of the location of politics, at a time when LGBTQI+* claims are being distorted and assimilated. We are in a difficult situation then. The repoliticizing of LGBTQI+* politics, to put it one way, opens up alliances with some other subjects and groups and, at the same time, it may bring about an expansion of the distance between associations and the subjects that they supposedly represent. To respond to that challenge, agendas and strategies must be well thought out and, especially, putting them into practice can be fundamental: starting initiatives, looking for alliances and articulations, and, although daunting, looking into empty spaces that may create transformative politics. Groups and initiatives will constantly be found between radical inner-looking intimacy and shared but dizzying spaces. Without ignoring the importance of symbolic politics, it will be essential to construct bridges that can connect those politics with some other dimensions by means of initiatives, diagnostics, ideas, and proposals.

To conclude, Leslie Feinberg's quote that began the chapter seems an appropriate metaphor. Jess is next to Stonewall, which is a very powerful symbol in LGBTQI+* politics, ready to take a photograph next to it. But the symbol is a bagel shop now. If that were not enough, then Jess will be witness to an extreme act of violence against a homeless transfeminine person, which will disturb him and almost no one else. The passage teaches us at least two interesting lessons. First, if our movement turns into a bagel shop, it will stop being helpful for people, for *all* LGBTQI+ people. Second, although past references are useful, the only option to move forward is (re)routing, looking in new, different directions.

BIBLIOGRAPHY

Ahmed, Sara. *Fenomenologia Queer: orientaciones, objetos, otros.* Barcelona: Bellaterra, 2019.

Bersani, Leo. *Homos.* Cambridge, MA: Harvard University Press, 1995.

Braidotti, Rosi. *Sujetos nómades: corporización y diferencia sexual en la teoría feminista contemporánea.* Buenos Aires, etc.: Paidós, 2000.

___. *Por una política afirmativa: itinerarios éticos.* Barcelona: Gedisa, 2018.

Charmaz, Kathy. *Constructing Grounded Theory.* Thousand Oaks, CA: Sage Publications, 2006.

Clarke, Adele. 2005. *Situational Analysis: Grounded Theory after the Postmodern Turn.* Thousand Oaks, CA: Sage Publications.

Day, Richard J.F. *De la hegemonía a la afinidad: solidaridad y responsabilidad en los nuevos movimientos sociales.* Madrid: Enclave de libros, 2016.

Deleuze, Gilles, and Félix Guattari. *Mil mesetas: capitalismo y esquizofrenia.* Valencia: Pre-Textos, 2002.

Duberman, Martin. *Stonewall, el origen de una revuelta.* Madrid: Ediciones Imperdible, 2018.

Egaña Etxeberria, Ibon. *"Queer literatura inguratuz."* %100 *Basque. Forum hitzaldiak,* zenb. 10, 2017: 67–78.

Epelde, Edurne, Miren Aranguren, and Iratxe Retolaza. *Gure genealogia feministak. Euskal Herriko mugimendu feministaren kronika bat.* Emagin Dokumentazio Zentrua, Pamplona, 2015.

Espinosa Miñoso, Yuderkis. "¿Hasta dónde nos sirven las identidades? Una propuesta de repensar la identidad y nuestras políticas deidentidaden los movimientos feministas y étnico-raciales." *Creatividad Feminista,* 1999.

Esposito, Roberto. *El dispositivo de la persona.* Buenos Aires; Madrid: Amorrortu, 2012.

Esteban, Mari Luz. "La reformulación de la política, el activismo y la etnografía. Esbozo de una antropología somática y vulnerable." *Ankulegi. Revista de Antropología Social,* zenb. 19, 2015.: 75–93.

Fraser, Nancy. *Scales of Justice: Reimagining Political Space in a Globalizing World.* New York: Columbia University Press, 2010.

Gamson, Joshua. "Messages of Exclusion: Gender, Movements, and Symbolic Boundaries." *Gender & Society* 11 (2), 1997: 178–99.

Hester, Helen. *Xenofeminismo: tecnologías de género y políticas de reproducción.* Buenos Aires: Cajanegra, 2018.

Joxemi Zumalabe Fundazioa. "Gatazkak. Borroka moldeak eta kultura politikoa herri mugimenduetan." Donostia: Joxemi Zumalabe Fundazioa, 2019.

Livia Alga, María. *Etnografía «terrona» de sujetos excéntricos.* Barcelona: Edicions Bellaterra, 2018.

López Romo, Raúl. *Del gueto a la calle: el movimiento gay y lesbiano en el País Vasco y Navarra, 1975–1983.* Donostia-San Sebastián: Tercera Prensa, 2008.

McIntyre, Alice. *Participatory Action Research.* SAGE Publications, 2008.

Montenegro, Marisela, and Marcel Balasch. "Una propuesta metodológica desde la epistemología de los conocimientos situados: las producciones narrativas." *Encuentros en Psicología Social* 1(3), 2003: 44-48.

Puar, Jasbir K. *Ensamblajes terroristas: el homonacionalismo en tiempos queer.* Barcelona: Bellaterra, 2017.

Rich, Adrienne. "Compulsory Heterosexuality and Lesbian Existence." *Signs* 5 (4), 1980: 631-60.

____. "Notes towards a politics of location." *Feminist postcolonial theory: A reader,* 1984: 29-42.

Spade, Dean. *Una vida «normal»: la violencia administrativa, la política trans crítica y los límites de derecho.* Barcelona: Bellaterra, 2015.

Stryker, Susan. *Historia de lo trans: las raíces de la revolución de hoy.* Madrid: Continta Me Tienes, 2017.

Taylor, Verta, and Nancy Whittier. "Collective Identity in Social Movement Communities, Lesbian Feminista Mobilization." In *Frontiers in Social Movement Theory,* Adon D. Morris eta Carol McClurg Mueller. Yale University Press, 1992.

Vidarte, Francisco Javier. *Ética marica: proclamas libertarias para una militancia LGTBQ.* Barcelona: Egales Editorial, 2007.

Zabala González, Begoña. *Movimiento de mujeres, mujeres en movimiento.* Tafalla: Txalaparta, 2008.

Notes

1 Throughout the article I will use the term LGBTQI+* politics, even though the term itself is awkward in the work. The activists and groups interviewed do not always identify their efforts and activities as LGBTQI+. Many of them prefer to define their group as TransQueerFag, or as transfeminist. Others do not see themselves as involved in LGBTQI+ activism, because they conceive of their efforts, precisely, within the field of transfeminism or lesbian feminism. For that reason, I will speak about LGBTQI+* politics and not the LGBTQI+ movement or activism. I would like to clarify that this expresses my personal choice, linked to my activist trajectory, and that the added asterisk does not just and mainly refer to those abbreviations that must be added to new terms, as is commonly understood (intersexual, queer . . .), but to the different forms that can be understood as transforming all those identities into political subjects (dyke, feminist lesbian, transfeminist, fag, trans* . . .), those that, de facto, locate the activists in different expressions of popular movements.

2 One should clarify that many participants, those who reject ranking within LGBTQI+* politics, see the last two rights, those that are some demands of the trans* collective, at different levels of achievement and therefore as still urgent.

3 From LGBTQI+, the term TMBB maintains trans* and Bi(sexual) in the name and replaces gay with fag and lesbian with dyke, seeking to neutralize the normalization of those identities. Those who use this term argue that the names gay and lesbian have been assimilated and that way they reclaim the curse words claiming their political potential for abjection. In his book *Homos*, Leo Bersani (1995) criticizes this position strongly, for different reasons, and some of the interviewees likewise do not support that policy of renaming.

4 For more on the historical perspective, see the already-cited López Romo (2008) and Epelde, Aranguren, and Retolaza (2015).

5 As I explained previously, these activists oppose the word "fag" to "gay." They say "gay" to a man who does not politicize his homosexuality. Not politicizing means just calling for respect for his choice, from an individual perspective, and understanding the gay experience as separate from any other vectors, without class, without race, without gender . . .

5

Intersexualities: Understanding Bodies beyond Binary Categories from a Biographical Perspective

María Gómez

Intersex activist and graduate student of the University of the Basque Country (EHU)

INTRODUCTION

In the current study, I intend to present a critical approach to the intersexualities category from autobiographic and scientific discourse. Intersexual people are born with sexual characteristics (testes, chromosomes, or genitals) that do not fit with the binary standard of the female or male. This reality has always existed, but it is important to understand that people called hermaphrodites in the past have gone through different modifications until being eliminated in the cultural and legal discourse. Bodies which have been subjected to revision and, moreover, which do not fit the norm, have been led to becoming objects of revision and punishment throughout history. Today, these people who challenge the legal, moral, theological, and biological rules continue to be the target of revision from a medical system that systematically corrects and intervenes in their bodies. Demonstrating the agency that we have had in recent years to incorporate some of our experiences into scientific understanding is one of the main objectives of this chapter.

AN APPROACH TO THE OBJECT OF STUDY. TO WHAT DO WE REFER WHEN WE SPEAK ABOUT INTERSEXUALITIES?

In this first section, I include some of the definitions that most approximate the form of understanding intersexualities from international intersex political and social activism. Moreover, I incorporate some proposals by academic researchers committed to this object of study.

I will start, therefore, by explaining the definition included on the website of one of the most renowned international bodies in the issue of the struggle for the rights of intersex people: the International Intersex Organization (OII):[1]

> Intersex people are born with atypical sex characteristics. Intersex relates to a range of congenital physical traits or variations that lie between stereotypical definitions of male and female. That is, physical differences in chromosomes, genetic expression, hormonal differences, reproductive parts like the testicles, penis, vulva, clitoris, ovaries, and so on. Many different forms of intersex exist; it is an umbrella term, rather than a single category. Intersex differences usually have a manifestation in primary or secondary sexual anatomy that is visible either externally or internally. We are intersex because our innate sex characteristics seem to be either male and female at the same time or not quite male or female or neither male nor female (http://oiiinternational.com/intersex-library/intersex-articles/what-is-intersex/ Consulted July 5, 2019).

This organization was founded by Curtis Hinkle and currently has centers and initiatives around the world such as OII Australia, represented by Gina Wilson; OII Europe,[2] with its representative Guillot; and with Dau García-Dauder as the representative of the Spanish state (Gregori, 2015: 108). For its part, OII China is known for its campaign *Free Hugs with Intersex,*[3] proposed by the activist Hiker Chiu[4]. OII South Africa is very committed to ending discrimination against the intersex collective. Some of their main demands are: a) Intersexed people are a natural variant and an important part of human diversity; b) The birth of an intersexed infant should be celebrated no less than the birth of any other infant; c) All diversity should be valued whether of race, culture, gender, sexual orientation, ability, geography, and or socio-economic status. Intersex South Africa (ISSA) advocates, mediates, and provides services for intersex people throughout South Africa. The objectives of ISSA are to advance intersexed people's rights through national legislation and service provision for intersexed people and their families. ISSA is responsible for creating open discussions and workshops on intersexuality for various organizations throughout South Africa. A primary goal of Intersex South Africa is to end nonconsensual, unnecessary genital surgery of all intersex people.[5]

Likewise, like the OII but from an academic and, for the first time, non-English-language position, Mauro Cabral brings us closer to the concept by making a brief historical summary of its evolution:[6]

> If we approach their possible meanings, we find a relatively new concept, certainly stripped of the stigma of its approximate synonyms; a term with almost no history, aseptically designating a certain fantastic disposition of the bodies, anchored at the same time in a tormented imagination and mythology; a rewriting in a politically correct key of the multiple conjugations of Victorian hermaphroditism, a collection of diverse alterations of the genitals of diverse origins, which is present in one in every two thousand births; a signal for the imperative and seemingly unappealable speed of surgical and hormonal intervention on the bodies of new-borns; an obligatory nod to the theories of John Money and its application in the history of medicine and the life of the people, the model that from psychiatry, pediatric urology, endocrinology, and surgery has normalized for decades, and normalizes, the "indecipherable" genitals of intersex people; the organized political movement of those same people, who openly defy the compulsive normalization of our identity and the need to make it literal over our bodies, returning to an ethical claim dispossessed by almost everyone almost everywhere, and yet today, again, in this place, wants to be heard: the fundamental respect for our autonomy (Cabral 2003, 118-119).

One of Cabral's contributions has been the incorporation of intersexuality into the international Human Rights agenda, in that of the ILGA (International Lesbian, Gay, Bisexual, Trans, and Intersex Association), ILGA Europe and other LGBTQI+ agendas to create a legal framework within international law. Likewise, Cabral is very critical of feminisms for not incorporating intersexualities as an objective, and of academics for *objectivizing* intersex people in their research (Gregori 2015, 105).

Another significant author in the field of law at the University of Granada is Daniel J. García. For this author, a hermaphrodite will always be that person born in a body over which another subject (a doctor, judge, civil registrar) decides that it is not a typical male or female body. An individual whose sex it is not possible to fit into the male/female normative binomial and that, for that very reason, calls into question the "natural" character of the duality of the sexes (García 2015, 60). Likewise, the philosopher Paul B. Preciado defines the intersexual body as that which is situated at the limits of the human. From an institutional point of view, it has no face or name, it is just an anus. As the author says, in denying the normative assignation of male or female it is intervened with and mutilated in infancy. This happens because socialization institutions (the family, school, state, and local administrations . . .) cannot function with a body that calls into question the binary categories of sex and gender with which they work (Preciado 2009, 168). From the field of medical anthropology, Nuria Gregori[7] defines intersexual people as those that are born with sexual characteristics, including genitals, reproductive anatomy, gonads, and chromosomes, which do not fit in with the typical binary notion of male and female bodies (2015). It is a term which is used to describe a wide variety of natural corporeal variations. In some cases, the features are visible at birth while in others, they are not discovered until puberty since many of them have no reason to be visible from an external perspective. Thus, taking into account that pointed out in the text "Los cuerpos ficticios de la biomedicina. El proceso de construcción del género en los protocolos médicos de asignación de sexo en bebés intersexuales":

> the external genital appearance may be sufficient to speak of intersexuality, regardless of whether or not there is organic dysfunction. Genital variability in this case is problematized, and consequently, is medicalized. In any case, the biomedical explanation of the normal process of sexual differentiation and of the problems or errors arising in this sequence transforms human sexual variability into pathological stages of genital ambiguity due to errors in development (Gregori, 2006).

On the other hand, there are a growing number of initiatives promoted by intersex activists at international meetings. Their goal would be to formulate some basic principles aimed at defending intersexual people. One of the most important initiatives was the Second International Intersex Forum in Stockholm on December 10, 2012. This historic event brought together thirty-seven activists that represented thirty-three intersex organizations and other support institutions from almost every continent. They pursued one common goal: standing up for the respect for the human rights of intersex people at the international, regional, and national level (Gregori 2015, 114). Likewise, the Second OII Europe Community Event

2019 was held in Zagreb, Croatia. It brought together intersex activists from all over the world with its main objectives: "political advocacy, health-related advocacy, and personal advocacy."[8]

HOW MANY PEOPLE ARE BORN INTERSEX?

How many babies are born intersex? We can never get a precise answer. It is difficult to calculate the average because of the invisibility of the topic and the lack of medical consensus to classify the different types of intersexuality. Even so, some authors have dared to offer approximate figures following their research. According to Gregori "between 0.05 percent and 1.7 percent of the population is born with intersexual features, the higher estimate would be similar to the number of redheaded people in the population" (Gregori, 2015). In the field of biology, Anne Fausto-Sterling (2006, 74) argues that 1.7 percent of all newborns in the world correspond to intersexual variations. This would mean that every year thousands of intersex babies are born in the world. Normally these data are typically used for comparison with the proportion of albino people since this is considered a human condition that is unusual to find. In any event, the proportion of intersex babies is usually greater than that of albino people. The data offered by Fausto-Sterling refer to hospital statistics, so the figure would increase if we take into account all those people who have not gone through medical processes. This is becoming more and more visible with the proliferation of collectives formed by international activists that fight for human rights. Thanks to them we are already beginning to get increasingly precise data. According to the Intersex Society of North America, in the United States, every year, one out of every 1,500-2,000 births is that of an intersexual baby (http://www.isna.org/faq/frequency consulted on April 5, 2019). Likewise, the website of the Organisation Intersex International Europe includes some data which affirm that the number of people that are born intersexual is one in every 200 people (https://www.youtube.com/watch?v=f4Z95e_aQBc consulted on April 5, 2019). Even so, the main problem continues to be, in Fausto-Sterling's words:

> instead of forcing ourselves to admit the social nature of our ideas over sexual difference, our increasingly sophisticated medical techniques have allowed us, in converting such bodies into male and female, to insist on the fact that people are, by nature,

either men or women, independent of the fact that intersex births may be noticeably frequent and may be growing (2006, 75).

GENEALOGY: FROM THE MYTH OF THE HERMAPHRODITE TO THE INTERSEXUALITIES OF TODAY

Up to the twentieth century, intersexual people were known culturally by the name of hermaphrodites. What was initially a myth would become flesh-and-bone people thereafter. The Roman poet Ovid, in book IV of *The Metamorphoses*, was already speaking about the history of Salmacis and Hermaphroditus. The bodies of the naiad and the son of Venus (Aphrodite) and Mercury (Hermes) joined together forever in one single body with two sexes. But when the androgynous figure abandons the field of myths and moves into the world of flesh and bone, in the words of García, "an inversion of values takes place" (García 2015, 25). In ancient Rome, it was permitted to kill a newborn who was malformed or had the characteristics of a monster. That monster would begin to challenge all legal, moral, theological, and biological norms and for that reason would have to be imprisoned. It was viewed as bad luck if a baby was born a hermaphrodite and it was sentenced to death through a purification ceremony (García 2015, 26-27). Later, tolerance increased, and they were even allowed to get married. In the *Digest* (I, 5, 10), Ulpian contends that the sex attributable to the hermaphrodite is that which may appear to dominate and they could participate in the institution of the testament if the male sex predominated. Thus, the hermaphrodite body acquired different moral and legal values over time, from being condemned to death by being burnt at the stake to living in accordance with the sex that most predominated within their body. Modernity, however, would be the epoch in which those sentences were reduced and the religious burden began to decline. The body that was subject to violence would begin to be a body that was examined, monitored, and regulated by institutions. According to Michel Foucault, a policy of punishment would be replaced by another in accordance with the new liberal times:

> an effort to adjust the mechanisms of power that frame the existence of individuals; an adaptation and a refining of the apparatuses which concern themselves with their everyday conduct, their identity, their activity, their apparently unimportant gestures, and they monitor them; a different policy with regard to the multiplicity of bodies and forces that make up a population (Foucault 2012, 91).

Even so, until the early twentieth century the dominant posture in medical knowledge was that only one sex existed. Galen's model (2 A.D.) understood that the woman was just an imperfect inversion of the dominant, male model. In this way, the vagina was conceived as an internal penis; the labia as the foreskin, the uterus as the scrotum, and the ovaries as the testicles (Thomas Laqueur 1994, 22). In his 1803 book *Historie Naturelle de la Femme,* Jacques Louis Moreau would implant the model of two differentiated sexes in body and soul. From this point on, biology was configured as the epistemological basis of the normative order (Laqueur 1994: 33). Since then and to this day, the penis has been transformed into a status symbol or would be the certificate that gives certain rights and privileges within the patriarchal system. By the same token, it was established that biologically, naturally, only two sexes existed: male and female. According to García, "binarism, ultimately, occupies the scene" (García 2015, 55).

Analyzing the medical history of intersexuality allows us to understand the changes in prevailing ideas about gender, both in Europe and in North America, as an heir to European medical traditions. One piece of data that stands out is that "doctors in Antiquity, who located sex and gender along a continuum and not in the discrete categories of today, were not perturbed by hermaphrodites" (Fausto-Sterling 2006, 51). From a scientific or medical point of view, hermaphrodites were considered as quantitative variations within a sexual continuum, and not as qualitative breaks which mark a chasm between the only two possible sexual options. For that reason, they were accepted as possibilities within human sexual variation. Likewise, it was not just doctors or biologists who had the authority and capacity to define and regulate the situation of hermaphrodites; jurists, too, and the different religions offered notions, laws, and norms about hermaphroditism up to the nineteenth century. There is evidence in different European legislation that, in spite of their distinct treatment, they coincide in one question: "the categorical distinction between male and female was at the core of legal and political systems" (2006: 52). Intersexual people were obliged to take a stance as a man or a woman and decide which sex they were going to live with and according to what they would be recognized and expressed in society.

We find a difference in the development of biology and technology. Both factors changed the way of understanding intersexual bodies. Fausto-Sterling states how, in the late eighteenth and early nineteenth centuries, biology took shape as a science, and varied its way of treating ambiguous bodies. Nineteenth-century scientists began to classify the births of bodies following statistics and, thus, established which type of corporealities were infrequent or abnormal. The birth of teratology in the nineteenth century, as the science which studied and classified unusual births, marked a new way of conceiving subjects that were born with anomalies. Ambiguous bodies would begin to be conceived as imperfections of nature which had to be corrected, and the classification system of corporeal varieties which was established made hermaphrodites disappear gradually from this system. The new classifications restricted the necessary characteristics to be able to be considered a hermaphrodite, and at the same time they did not contemplate the existence of people of mixed or ambiguous sex. This process culminated in the mid-twentieth century with the development of endocrinology and the possibility of intervening surgically on bodies and adapting them to a male or female body—a model that remains to this day.

The birth of endocrinology would bring with it a change of paradigm: if previously subjects could decide to which legal sex they wished to belong, maintaining at least the ambiguity of their bodies, from the twentieth century on intersex subjects themselves would be able to decide about their bodies, and if not, it would be doctors who, faced with the birth of a baby, would decide to which sex it would belong, correcting imperfections in nature. The possibility of remaining in an intersexual or ambiguous corporeal state disappeared with technological advances, and every subject had to fit into the dualist model of sexed bodies, "as curable aberrations according to increased medical knowledge" (Fausto-Sterling 2006, 55).

In the 1950s in the United States, John Money and his colleagues at Johns Hopkins University began to publish their research. Their main contribution defended the idea that gender identity is neutral at birth and in early infancy, being determined subsequently by the genitals and upbringing. Gender identity would be the exclusive product of upbringing and socialization. The role of genitals would be secondary as a marker. According to this theory, the child's mind would be like an empty blackboard and without any inherent personality characteristics, while gender identity would depend on the education received. In this way, people would begin to forge a consciousness of their own sex from the age of eighteen months, this being conditioned by learning (Fausto-Sterling

2006, 46-77). Money understood that intersexual minors had to subject themselves to surgical processes to correct their genitality and thus develop a stable gender identity to guarantee their physical and psychological well-being. Therefore, the group at Johns Hopkins University was charged with creating the protocols that still, today, prevail in the event an intersexual baby is born.

If we turn to the context of the Spanish state, already in the 1930s, another doctor began to speak about a chemical conception of sex/gender that explained that what pushed us to behave or to desire in a specific way depends on the type and quantity of the hormones there are in an organism. Gregorio Marañón recognized in his work *Evolucion de la sexualidad y los estados intersexuales,* published in 1930, that a phase of undifferentiated sexuality exists as a starting point of all human beings and introduces the idea of sex as a *continuum.* For him, the difference between the sexes is established as a scale between two extremes, in which most people locate themselves:

> Almost no human presents wholly pure sexual signs [. . .] detailed observation will discover, almost without exception, the trace of the "other sex," which persists in a group of features, morphological (the distribution of bodily and head hair, the development of the larynx, the proportions of the skeleton, etc.) or functional (libido, social conduct, character, sensibility, voice, etc.) (Marañón 1928, 259).

Although his contributions would help to resist a strict biological dualism between sexes, he himself would later label hermaphrodite people with the same pathological categories that would serve to identify problems within that scale of gradations created. This idea would be seen in his later definition of the "deviations," the "defects," the anomalies, and the different "problems" which were established in sexual differentiation and which underpinned "intersexual states." Indeed, these theories prevail today; the "idea of the continuum in sex" and the presumption of hormonal duality; oestrogen for women and testosterone for men—although a little later it would be discovered that all humans share all the hormones in variable quantities (Gregori 2015, 46). In this way, there is still a justification of a treatment of surgical and hormonal normalization in all people that are born with characteristics that do not match the binary norm of the male and the female.

At this moment, there are three distinct positions in relation to intersexualities. There are professionals who still follow to the letter Money's protocols and, therefore, favor surgery as the only method to resolve the matter. In an intermediary position are those professionals, families, and patients who still believe in creating networks in the field of medicine to improve protocols of attention, working on bioethical questions, and educating health professionals. In the third group, we find people who defend the notion that the issues that threaten intersexual people are very closely related to sociopolitical interests, with rigid concepts such as assignation of sex, sex/gender, male or female. From that position, only one legal and political solution can remedy the discrimination and the lack of human rights for this collective (Gregori 2015, 2).

With all the opinions and positions on the table, the most straightforward thing to do is explain here the results of the work that I have been conducting on this topic. From that basis, I will mention the experience that has led me to favor, to some extent, the opinions of these three differentiated groups. To be able to debate and contribute from my body as an intersexual woman will allow me to explain my perspective on the topic, which does not attempt to be either more or less valuable than others, but which is equally necessary.

A BIOGRAPHICAL APPROACH TO INTERSEXUALITIES

In this section, I will try to offer a genealogy of my corporeal trajectory in the study of intersexualities that will allow us to continue delving into the object of study in this chapter, which is just one more step in a piece of ongoing research. The objective in this section is to draw attention to the activism which has been taking place in the Spanish state in recent years. Although there is still no intersex collective which represents the state at the international level, such as those which I have already mentioned in other countries,[10] there is an important and increasingly popular support group, GrApSIA.[11] Moreover, for some years important actions have been carried out at the individual level by intersex activists in different regions and cities in the state.

I am among those involved in this activism, in academia and at the social level. For that reason, I intend to explain a personal genealogy of my relationship with activism through my body as an intersex woman. To do so, in this section I am going to distinguish three different stages which sum up my trajectory in regard to intersexualities: a) First stage:

Meetings and mix-ups; b) Second stage: (De)construction and Agency; c) Third stage: I, intersex.

First Stage: Meetings and Mix-Ups

I will journey back to 2015, the moment in which I decided to study for a master's in international studies on peace, conflicts, and development at the Universidad Jaume I de Castelló (Spain). My experience in that master's, which lasted two academic years, gave me the opportunity to learn from other ways, other forms. It taught me to reflect, and reflect on myself as a human being; to think about the plurality of people, of stories, of cultures, of forms of teaching, and ways of learning. In addition to equipping me with new understandings, I was able to share experiences and theoretical discussions with people from many other places in the world. Being trained as a peacemaker—*peace functionaries*[12]—meant blending for months with people from the five continents and receiving an education with an intercultural, feminist, and cross-disciplinary perspective that changed my way of seeing and letting myself be seen in the world. Above all, it changed my way of looking at others. For the first time, I understood the meaning of certain concepts such as intersectionality, decolonialism, ethnocentrism, androcentrism, otherness, and interculturality. For the first time, I did so by accepting the privileges that allowed me to be there and the lack of them on getting more deeply involved in the study of my own particularity.

The master's, its people, the context, a blend of everything, led me to find an object of study that ran through me directly and a professional objective which dismantled everything that, to that point, I possessed in my imaginary. Being introduced theoretically to feminist studies via peace studies implied delving into my body to observe the intersections inscribed there and starting to deconstruct it.

Nor would this work of retrospection and analysis have been possible if at the associative level I had not had a space and a group in and with which to share my curiosities. For months I was able to get involved directly with a feminist collective in which I found colleagues for life who taught me how necessary collective activism was to try to change things and shed some light on a topic as necessary as respect for equality and diversity.

Being conscious of my intersections invited me to know other realities that helped me to not feel alone and to see a little bit of light at the end of the tunnel. In this way, in May 2016, I went to Barcelona to meet one of the researchers in the Spanish state who had most explored the subject of intersexualities, Nuria Gregori. We met at the Second Congress European Rainbow Cities. That meeting marked a point of inflection in my life to become fully involved in the study of intersexualities. It made me understand that that topic of study which crossed through me had many faces that I would recognize/understand with time. At the same conference, for the first time, I put a face and voice to more people who had gone through similar experiences to mine. I began to feel that I had to make visible my personal situation. If I dared do it, other people could take the same step. Thus, I developed my first research project through my final-year master's project: *Intersexualidades: entender los cuerpos más allá de las categorías binarias desde los Estudios para la Paz* (Intersexualities: Understanding bodies beyond binary categories from Peace Studies) (Gómez, 2016).

Once the object of study had been chosen, it was clear that I wanted to include the life stories of some of the people whom I had gotten to know at that time. That motivation led me to search for methodological proposals that might allow me to collect these voices, and it was then that I came across the methodological and epistemological approaches of Donna Haraway[13] (1995, 251-311) on situated knowledges. Haraway reclaims the need for partiality to create out of particularity and from an embedded and situated position (1995, 339): "we do not seek partiality in itself, but for the unexpected connections and openings that situated knowledges make possible" because "the only way of finding a broader perspective is to be in a place in particular."

In that first approach to the field of the research, two people wanted to share their testimonies: Covadonga and Bárbara.[14] The two participants were diagnosed in adolescence (in the 1990s and the 2000s respectively) with Morris' syndrome or testicular feminization syndrome, now known clinically as androgen insensitivity syndrome. They had grown up having a normative phenotype expected of a woman's body. They had been raised to that moment as such, yet the analyses demonstrated that they had an XY karyotype (a karyotype that, according to the binary sexual model, matched that of a male). The androgen insensitivity syndrome is the cause of a "hereditary change in the testosterone recipient on the cellular surface" and its basic clinical features,

> are XY babies with very feminized genitals. The body is blind to
> the presence of testosterone, given that the cells cannot receive it

and use it to direct development via the male way. In puberty these intersexes develop breasts and a female outline" (Fausto-Sterling 2006, 71).

In the face of these diagnostics in most cases, and following the Money protocol, intersexual minors must subject themselves to surgical processes to correct their genitality and thereby develop a gender identity that guarantees their physical and psychological well-being. In the case of Bárbara they acted by following the same procedure. As she explains, "those of us that have Morris' syndrome have to be operated on because instead of ovaries we have two gonads that have not ended up developing and, according to the doctors, they can create a tumour." Covadonga, because she was of legal age when they discovered her diagnosis, was given the option of choosing whether to remove her gonads or not. She decided not to do so, now more than three decades ago.

Other cases of intersex people are detected at the moment of birth, especially when "anomalies" are perceived in the genitals. According to clinical protocols, there are genitals which do not match the indicated averages and, for that reason, they must be corrected: "we know that the average clitoris of newborns measures 0.345 cm while more recent studies demonstrate that the averages of a normal-sized clitoris vary between 0.2 cm and 0.85 cm, as can be observed in phallometry" (Fausto-Sterling 2006, 72). In the case of Covadonga and of Bárbara, their genitals were within the averages indicated by these scales. For that reason, their intersexuality was not detected at the moment of birth but instead from their hormonal and sexual development onward.

As already noted, intersexualities do not refer to identities but, rather, they are biological sexual characteristics, which is something different to sexual orientation, to its gender identity. An intersexual person can be heterosexual, gay, lesbian, bisexual, or asexual. Equally, they may identify as a woman, as a man, both or neither. Covadonga feels like a woman and is in a relationship with another woman. Bárbara, for her part, defines herself as bisexual and as an intersexual woman; intersexual on account of her biology and a woman as the gender with which she expresses herself and feels.

Lastly, one of the common elements of their two stories was silence. One that is repeated time and time again in each experience. This silence is determined by medical discourse. Both Bárbara and Covadonga demonstrate through their words the solitude to which they were subjected in adolescence because of the silence with which they lived. Bárbara told us how "in one way or another I felt like I couldn't speak, that if I did speak, I'd be rejected, that if there was no information about that it's because the people I met like me had not spoken either." Covadonga, because she was a public figure, was barred from speaking and advised to lie about her situation. Years later she continues to struggle for her rights without anyone shutting her up. Currently, both advocate for a greater visibility on all levels and in all areas, and they work actively within the academic environment in favor of the rights of intersex people.

Likewise, within the realm of political and social activism, some months after defending and publishing my final-year master's project (2016), I decided to write my own history, adapt it to be dramatized and stage it. That is how Lola was born. Every afternoon during the summer of 2016, Lola got up on stage, sat down on a chair in front of her audience, and began her work: "I'm Lola, I'm intersexual, and I'm going to tell you my story." For the first time, I was able to overcome the silence and talk in front of the people who had come to see my monologue. It was, without any doubt, an exercise in empowerment and freedom. I felt freer than ever being able to recount everything that I could not say before, and doing so without anyone pointing at me or judging me; protected by a pseudonym that was ultimately my salvation. Lola did not stop there, but instead some months later I adapted the monologue into a press article for *Pikara Magazine*, an online feminist journal (Bilbo, Bizkaia): https://www.pikaramagazine.com/2017/03/soy-lola-y-soy-intersexual/# Accessed July 6, 2019).

SECOND STAGE: (DE)CONSTRUCTION AND AGENCY

In 2017, one year later, a set of coincidences took me to the Basque Country to study and continue in my political activism. I had the opportunity to collect knowledge and theoretical contributions in feminist studies, participating as a student in a master's course on feminist and gender studies at the University of the Basque Country (UPV/EHU). I also got involved, with my now thesis advisor Jone Miren Hernández, in a project for the Comprehensive Attention for Minors with a Different Sexual Development proposed by the pediatric surgery team at the Donosti Hospital (Gipuzkoa), in which we are still participating. At the same time, I also published a press report, once again, for *Pikara*

Magazine. This new report, "La I está empezando a salir del armario" ("The I is beginning to come out of the closet"),[15] reflects on the agency of five intersex women who, in the same way as Lola, sought to make themselves visible and come out of the closet.

In the first place, I will speak about the work undertaken to date for the project for the Comprehensive Attention for Intersex Minors in the Basque Country. One of the first clinical teams in the Spanish state to create a multidisciplinary working group incorporating the gender perspective into its project has been OSI Donostialdea (Donostia, Gipuzkoa). Its goal is to broaden sanitary protocols. To do so, it has been proposed to explore new areas of knowledge that also take into account the feminist perspective on topics related to bodies and sexuality. This is titled: Attention for Minors with a Different Sexual Development, and it is a project of integrated attention centered on patients requested by the team of professionals itself. Its starting date was September 1, 2017, and its closing date is still to be determined. The pediatric surgery team at the OSI Donostialdea is in charge.[16] The participating and collaborating organizations are: (1) pediatric surgery service at OSI Donostialdea; (2) IIS Biodonostia service; (3) the pediatric endocrinology units at OSI Donostialdea, OSI Eskerraldea-Enkarterri-Cruces, and OSI Araba; (4) and the master's in feminist and gender studies program at UPV/EHU.[17]

The project's objective is to conduct a retrospective revision of the documented cases to date of minors with a different sexual development (DSD) in the Basque Autonomous Community and also to collect the evaluation of the assistance received in each of the cases. It is intended to create a comprehensive, interdisciplinary, and coordinated assistance circuit, which accompanies the pubescent, psychological, sexual, and social development of minors, identifying individualized assistance needs in every moment. The methodology to be used is a bibliographic search of the different assistance approaches and the legislative bases; a retrospective descriptive study of the DSD cases diagnosed; and the incorporation of the gender perspective to give the power of decision to the families. The people in the study are minors who have been diagnosed by pediatric endocrinology services.

Our mission has consisted of elaborating on surveys that have been completed by the families of the minors during one of their medical visits in the participating hospitals. We wrote the survey questions, incorporating the suggestions of health and sociology researchers. Our aim was to get it as complete as possible to obtain the most information from families and to learn their principal needs. Once the survey was concluded, it served as a reference to contextualize it within the field of feminist studies.[18] Giving a qualitative point of view and a closer perspective to the theoretical-methodological proposals in feminist anthropology was our objective. It was also an objective in the elaboration of the final-year master's project that I will mention below.

This second project has been one more piece in the puzzle that I have been completing in diverse areas. Likewise, it has served to focus my principal objective in regard to the next collaborations: transform intersexual people into subjects of study and into agents generating their (our) own discourses. In this way and employing theoretical knowledge, having meetings with more intersex people and applying feminist qualitative methodological tools, I completed my second final-year master's project, "Intersexualidades: conversaciones entre madres e hijas. Un acercamiento teórico-metodológico a los cuerpos no binaries" (Intersexualities: conversations between mothers and daughters. A theoretical-methodological approach to non-binary bodies) (Gómez, 2018).[19]

In this second final-year project, my principal interest consisted of recovering the voices of three intersex people and their mothers to bring their stories to the center of the debate.[20] Thus, through six semi-structured interviews, I learned first-hand their needs, the relationship with their bodies on the basis of the diagnosis, their evaluation of the comprehensive assistance received, and the processes experienced between then and now. I have been able to listen to their experiences and delve more deeply into their life stories. Likewise, the research has allowed me to reflect on the agency that these people are beginning to have right now. And all of this was done in order to not make the same mistakes. The idea of bringing the voices of their mothers to the center of the debate and building a dialogue on the basis of the contributions of each and every one of them has implied a personal challenge for them and for me as the researcher. Thanks to this collective experience with intersexual women, I have understood that working together, at the same level, creating collective imaginaries and meanings, avoiding power relations, and talking from partiality is, today, completely necessary. Their contributions have been essential to continue participating in future multidisciplinary projects and thereby contributing to generating more exhaustive, inclusive, and plural knowledge with this collective.

The three people who participated in the final-year master's project together with their mothers, Maia, Cristina, and Alek, also form part of the press report "La I está empezando a salir del armario." Alongside them and two other intersex women, Lilith and Violeta, we collectivize our experiences to make them visible in *Pikara Magazine* (Bizkaia). To draw this up, we invigorate a dialogue among the five, focusing on the form of experiencing gender and sexuality, the relationship with our bodies, with feminism and with the LGTBI movement. On this basis, we called for collective responsibility to continue creating new imaginaries that may make visible other bodies and other forms of being possible. Placing at the center of the debate some of these contributions in this report reflects the activism that has been undertaken in recent years in the Spanish state. Likewise, the conclusions in the above-mentioned report go along with those obtained in the final-year master's project. For that reason, I would like to include here some ideas that were put on the table:[21]

> "Imagine that they diagnose you with a syndrome, which you always had and which very few people have, they remove a gonad out of the fear it may produce a tumor and they tell you that you don't have a uterus, or ovaries, nor will you ever have a period, nor are you fertile. Fourteen years old. Manage it." LOLA
>
> "At first, my body perception was incomplete, it didn't fit, the scars after the operations didn't help, I didn't consider myself a real woman and in my family it was normalized as a taboo, by means of silence." TRECE
>
> "Although in binary terms I identify as a woman, we must keep working on the queer dimension in order to leave behind the discriminatory sexual dualism and gender roles." LILITH

The image Cristina describes in her discourse on how she experienced puberty is very revealing to understand the influence of the binary sexual model in Western societies: "When I didn't get my period, and on realizing that it was XY, that I had a blind vagina, and internal feminized testicles, there was a short circuit in my brain: What am I? What is this farce? What are other people going to think? I didn't feel worthy of being a woman or of introducing myself as such." Violeta affirmed that both the patriarchy and the influence of the Catholic religion in our society have made her feel like a "third division woman." This feeling is shared by all of them, since in these five cases they were socialized from their birth as women. Silence and the relationships with the binary categories have been their main weapons of resistance.

The five experienced the removal of gonads, which is recommended in a general way and which now is beginning to be called into question, within and outside hospitals. According to Lola, "there is a whole normative apparatus which legitimizes those practices and which tells us which bodies, which genitals, which identities, or which sexual options are valid and which are not." For that reason, looking toward the future, they consider it essential to work for an interdisciplinary focus within and outside hospitals, aimed more at a socio-educational and cultural intervention and sensibilization.

Support groups already exist, but those I interviewed are convinced that making intersexuality more visible is fundamental to feel accepted. Some advocate creating associations without "pathologized perspectives" and weaving a support network among intersex people aimed at sharing experiences and creating changes at all levels: legislative, sanitary, and educational. They support the proliferation of intersex collectives and associations, and so that the "I" is present in the struggle for LGTBIQ+ rights and forming part of the feminist agenda. Other people, however, see it as fundamental to continue working on the collaboration with professionals, families, and patients and creating links with the field of medicine. Moreover, the need to improve attention protocols, work on basic questions, and educate health professionals is underscored.

THIRD STAGE: I, INTERSEX
With this final stage I attempt to conclude the chapter since it represents my most up-to-date present and is just a continuity of everything stated to this point. I am working on my PhD in the feminist and gender studies program at the EHU (Basque Country). I am conducting research that attempts to amplify all those intersex people who may want to participate in it. The idea is to continue advocating this route, the struggle for human rights and the visibility of our political cause in the sociocultural panorama. Moreover, from the social area I continue my collaboration with the journal *Pikara*, publishing an interview with a French intersex activist whose goal is to forge closer ties with international activism. Likewise, I am part of the support group GrApSIA, and I am giving more talks and courses in different cities in the Spanish state. All of these tasks are aimed at continuing to make our struggle visible.

Therefore, I would like to highlight the different perspectives that exist at the international level—and explained by Gregori (2015)—with regard to how to work on intersexualities. I champion the existence of legal and political solutions that advocate a break with the binary sexual model and the construction of new inclusive categories. Sex, gender, and/or sexuality are social and cultural constructions. Understanding this affirmation will allow us to feel freer when it comes to identifying ourselves, expressing ourselves, and defining ourselves with one or other of the concepts. To do so, it is necessary to continue fighting the discrimination which we still suffer as a collective and for the human rights of intersex minors who are still subjected to genital mutilations only for aesthetic and not strictly health reasons. Despite the fact that this is my main demand today, I also defend the idea that to achieve this objective, it is necessary to create networks with different disciplines and areas, such as medicine. It is still essential that intersex people, families, and health professionals work together to improve attention protocols and work on bioethical issues based on our main demands and needs. For that reason, I am part of the previously mentioned Comprehensive Attention project for minors. I am convinced the protocols will continue to change, that there will be more information, and that the alternatives given to families in medical consultations should be increasingly varied, free, and less imposed.

I conclude the chapter with this reflection, hoping that my contribution might imply a step forward at the scientific, political, and social level. Likewise, the diffusion of these reflections is a challenge which, in this case, will come into focus in the exchange of knowledge between the University of the Basque Country and the University of Nevada, Reno. All of this is to continue advocating new networks that foster relationships from an interdisciplinary, intercultural, and international perspective and favor the proliferation of theoretical discourses on intersexualities and human rights on the basis of our agency.

BIBLIOGRAPHY

Cabral, Mauro. "Pensar la intersexualidad, hoy." in *Sexualidades migrantes: género y transgénero* edited by Diana Maffía, 117-126. Buenos Aires: Feminaria, 2003.

Fausto-Sterling, Anne. *Cuerpos sexuados* Barcelona: Melusina, 2006.

Foucault, Michel. *Vigilar y Castigar.* Madrid: Siglo XXI, 1998.

———, *Herculine Barbin llamada Alexina B.* Madrid: Talasa, 2007.

Galé Moyano, María José. *Cuerpos Singulares, una lectura desde el pensamiento de Judith Butler,* Barcelona: Edicions Bellatera, 2013.

García, Daniel J. *Sobre el derecho de los hermafroditas.* Madrid: Melusina, 2015.

Gómez, María. "Intersexualidades: conversaciones entre madres e hijas. Un acercamiento teórico-metodológico a los cuerpos no binarios," Master's Thesis, Euskal Herriko Unibertsitatea, Euskal Herria (inédito) 2018.

———, "La I está empezando a salir del armario," *Pikara Magazine,* Consultado el 15 de abril de 2019 disponible en http://www.pikaramagazine.com/2018/04/dialogo-intersexualidad/ 2018.

———, "Soy Lola y soy Intersexual," *Pikara Magazine,* Consultado el 15 de abril de 2019, disponible en https://www.pikaramagazine.com/2017/03/soy-lola-y-soy-intersexual/#, 2017.

———, "Intersexualidades. Entender los cuerpos más allá de las categorías binarias desde los Estudios para la Paz," Tesis Doctoral, Universitat Jaume I de Castelló, Castelló (inédito) 2016.

Gregori, Nuria, "Encuentros y des-encuentros en torno a las intersexualidades/DSD: Narrativas, Procesos y Emergencias," Tesis Doctoral, Universitat de Valencia, Valencia (inédito) 2015.

———, "Los cuerpos ficticios de la biomedicina. El proceso de construcción del género en los protocolos médicos de asignación de sexo en bebés intersexuales," *AIBR: Revista de Antropología Iberoamericana,* 1(1), 2006: 103-124.

Haraway, Donna. *Ciencia, cyborgs y mujeres. La reinvención de la Naturaleza,* Cátedra, Madrid, 1995: p. 251-311.

Laqueur, Thomas. *La construcción del sexo, cuerpo y género desde los griegos hasta Freud,* Madrid: Cátedra, 1994.

Marañón, Gregorio. "Nuevas ideas sobre el problema de la intersexualidad y sobre la cronología de los sexos." *Revista de Occidente,* 6(66), p. 259, 1928.

Martínez, Vincent. "La filosofía de la Paz y el compromiso público de la filosofía," *Teoría de la Paz, Valencia: Nau Llibres,* 1995.

Vázquez, Francisco y Andrés Moreno. "Un solo sexo. Invencion de la monosexualidad y expulsion del hermafroditismo (España, siglos XV-XIX)," *Daimon. Revista de Filosofia,* 11, 1995.

NOTES

1 OII Intersex Network: http://oiiinternational.com
2 OII Europe website: https://oiieurope.org
3 See the following link: https://sogicampaigns.org/portfolio/a-hug-a-day-keeps-hate-away-free-hugging-in-taiwan/
4 See the following link: https://ilga.org/intersex-steering-committee-Asia
5 OII South Africa website: http://www.intersex.org.za/about-us/
6 Argentinian activist for the rights of intersex people.
7 Gregori, Nuria (2015): Encuentros y des-encuentros en torno a las intersexualidades/DSD: Narrativas, Procesos y Emergencias, Doctoral Thesis, Universitat de Valencia, Valencia (unpublished).
8 See the following link: https://oiieurope.org/es/welcome-to-the-3rd-oii-europe-community-event-conference-2019/
9 IGLYO (The International Lesbian, Gay, Bisexual, Transgender, Queer & Intersex Youth and Student Organisation) teamed with OII Europe-The International

Intersex Organisation Europe to answer some common questions about being intersex in video on YouTube.

10 See again: http://oiiinternational.com

11 Grupo de Apoyo al Síndrome de Insensibilidad a los Andrógenos (the Support Group for the Insensibility Syndrome toward Androgens) and related syndrome: https://grapsia.org

12 Martínez, Vincent (1995), "La filosofía de la Paz y el compromiso público de la filosofía," *Teoría de la Paz, Valencia: Nau Llibres, 77.*

13 Haraway, Donna (1995), Ciencia, cyborgs y mujeres. La reinvención de la Naturaleza, Cátedra, Madrid, 251-311.

14 The testimonies of Bárbara and Covadonga that are demonstrated in this section are included in the final-year master's project I completed in 2016 for the Universidad de Castelló: *Intersexualidades: entender los cuerpos más allá de las categorías binarias desde los Estudios para la Paz* (Gómez, 2016)

15 Gómez, María (2018), "La I está empezando a salir del armario," http://www.pikaramagazine.com/2018/04/dialogo-intersexualidad/ *Pikara Magazine,* accessed 17 August 17, 2018.

16 The person in charge (IP) of the project is the pediatric surgeon Dr. Nerea González Temprano at the OSI Donostialdea (Gipuzkoa).

17 The master's would be represented by the doctor in anthropology, Jone Miren Hernández, and myself, María Gómez, as a student in the doctoral program in feminist and gender studies.

18 We have still not been able to observe and study the data obtained in the surveys, which we hope will be published shortly by the same collaborative bodies.

19 Gómez, María (2018), "Intersexualidades: conversaciones entre madres e hijas. Un acercamiento teórico-metodológico a los cuerpos no binario." Final-year master's project.

20 The proposal that the mothers should participate alongside their daughters in the final-year master's project emerged as a response to some of the needs observed in prior conversations. Collecting the meetings and mix-ups between mothers and daughters—on account of the fact of *being* and *feeling like women* from their different bodies—to bring them to the center of the debate, became our main objective.

21 All the testimonies mentioned in this section are included in the report "La I está empezando a salir del armario": http://www.pikaramagazine.com/2018/04/dialogo-intersexualidad/ in Pikara Magazine.

6

Lesbianism and the Political Subject of the Feminist Movement in the Basque Country (1977-1994)

Maialen Aranguren

Experiencia Moderna Research Group (UPV/EHU)

INTRODUCTION

Nowadays the feminist movement is strong. The celebrations of International Women's Day (March 8) the last two years, the #MeToo movement, the extended #YoTeCreo ("Believe women") or #Cuéntalo campaigns are just some significant examples of that strength. One of the reasons of the success of the current feminist movement is the nature of its political subject. According to the words published in the dossier developed by the Basque Feminist Movement for the strike of March 2019, the political subjects of today's movement are:

"Women, lesbians, and trans, that is, the subjects oppressed by the heteropatriarchy.[1] (...) When we use the word woman*, we are referring to the subjects oppressed by the heteropatriarchy. We are non-salaried and salaried workers, unemployed, students, and pensioners. (...)

We are diverse and different oppression axes cross among us (...). We claim lesbian and trans identities as political positions, as ways to stand against the heteronormativity."[2]

The *woman* that the current Basque feminist movement has as its political subject, we can conclude from this quote, has a diverse identity and body, which is understood in a plural and not-excluding way.

That is where the most novel key of contemporary feminism lies, the qualitative jump given in the theoretical field and the ability to carry it to the streets. The atomization that prevailed in the postmodern context and which was considered as a weakness in the 1990s, has now become a unifying force. Recognizing the diversity of oppression axes and their complex intersections, the meaning of the category of woman was questioned. Besides deconstructing and extending it, the sexed body that is supposed to correspond to it, is not taken for granted and it has been situated in the center of the debate. But it has not always been that way. What is considered the success of the current feminist movement—the making of a deep and radical deconstruction of the bodies, which drove us to recognize an identity category constituted by different subjectivities—has its basis in a previous period, and that is what I will study.

In this text, I will focus on the discursive frameworks of the Basque Feminist movement and Emakumearen Sexual Askatasunerako Mugimendua (ESAM)[3] and lesbian collectives (they cannot be understood separately) that materialized from the second half of the 1970s. I will take into account the political meaning given to the *woman* and *lesbian* identities constituted by those discourses. I will precisely examine the evolution of the subject of the feminist movement created in those years of the Transition and the great influence that the figure of the lesbian had on it.[4]

The femininity ideal that originated from Francoism was the starting point of the feminist movement created in the second half of the 1970s. The Francoist regime, through different means, imposed a rigid and monolithic model of being woman and man. As in the case of other fields, gender relationships experienced changes during the Francoist dictatorship. Especially from the 1960s, starting from new discourses, gender relationships transformed and the possibilities of the femininity ideal extended. However, marriage, motherhood, and domesticity continued being the main referents for many women and to some extent, they were strengthened.[5] Many experts have stated that the feminist movement of the Transition was created as response to that femininity ideal.[6] Precisely, in that context, the feminists did a new reading about the femininity ideal that was in force. That reinterpretation was done in terms of oppression, overturning in a radical way the meaning of the inherited category of woman, without questioning the body that contained that new meaning. In this sense, and as we will see later, in those years the autonomous Basque feminist movement organized around a one-meaning strong political subject, the *woman*.[7] That category of woman had a universal nature; in that way, the idea that all the women suffered the same main oppression predominated, patriarchal oppression precisely, and, at the same time, they would share the same interests and the same fight. The gender was the main axis of the oppression of women and what united all of them together. However, by the end of the mentioned decade, and especially throughout the 1980s, some voices that did not identify completely with that reflection appeared from the inside of the movement. The lesbians affirmed they were crossed by another oppression axis and, in that way, the strong and uniform category of woman started to fracture until the diversity broke it in the 1990s. Along with that, the movement that was strong in the previous years became a skeletal structure.

WOMEN OF THE WORLD, UNITE!
In the second half of the 1970s thousands of women occupied the streets in Spain, demanding women's rights. In the context of Spain, a few weeks after the dictator Franco died, the First Conference for the Liberation of Woman took place in Madrid in secrecy. It was the first milestone of the movement. Five months later, the emerging feminist movement celebrated in Barcelona the First Catalan Conference of the Woman (1976).

Coming to our context, the autonomous Basque feminist movement started materializing in 1976. At that time, hundreds of Basque feminists were organized in groups called Assemblies of Women and by 1977 a wide net of the assemblies that gathered women of different groups and trends of the Basque Country had been woven. In December of that year they celebrated the First Conference of Basque Women. It could be said that those conferences held in Leioa (Biscay) were the foundational milestone of the autonomous movement. In truth, about 3,000 women took to the streets, giving visibility to the movement among Basque society.[8] There they debated about different issues, such as, sexuality, militancy models, or housework. Through those debates they knocked over the normative meanings of the world and were assigning new meanings, and, at the same time, founded the political subject of the movement. In this sense, the conferences were very significant emotional and discursive frameworks, as I will next explain, because it was then and there that a foundationalist fiction was founded.[9] It must not be forgotten that in that political context, of the transition from dictatorship to democracy, the possibilities to build the present and the future extended in a significant way. The women took part in that construction interpellating the whole of society. As I mentioned, so many authors have argued that the feminist movement of the Transition was a response to the Francoist femininity ideal. Thus, feminists did a new reading based on oppression about the femininity that was in force, giving a new political meaning to the category of woman inherited from Francoism.

On the other hand, the analysis of the debates of these conferences shows us that the autonomous Basque feminist movement of the Transition was plural and unified, both from an ideological perspective and from a perspective of the oppression of the woman. In general, three theoretical trends predominated in the Basque context: the feminism of the double militancy or equality; that of the only militancy or independent; and finally, the feminism of the difference. But, as it will be seen in the following pages, beyond the approach or different perspectives of those currents, all of them articulated a strong, coherent, and homogeneous political subject.

First of all, those in favor of the double militancy, in addition to being members of the movement of women, took part in political parties of the left and in trade unions. Their postulates had a basis in the Marxist theoretical framework, although they did a critical, feminist reading of those. Marxism's classic idea said that the main contradiction of women was the one they had within capitalism and that only the destruction of that system would be able to make disappear the material bases of the oppression of women. But, the members of this current, especially Trotskyists and Maoists, questioned the idea that the liberation of women was subordinated to the class struggle As denounced by women of Euskadiko Mugimendu Komunista (EMK),[10] the revolutionary parties put the emancipation of women unfairly subordinated to the working class struggle.

In front of that classic perspective, the double militants recognized that women suffered specific oppression. In their opinion, the sexual division of labor based on the patriarchal system was the reason for the oppression of women, one of the main contradictions of the women, indeed. In that system, the women were responsible for the reproduction function of workforce and household chores, and men benefited from that situation. In this sense, the proletarian women suffered a double oppression, as salaried workers and for their condition as women.[11] Thus, the women of bourgeois class were also oppressed for being women, despite living better conditions.[12] Therefore, the patriarchal oppression was the union bond among the women of different social classes.

The women of this current affirmed that the discourse that predominated in their parties about the social classes left aside the specific oppression of women, that it hid the bonds among them.[13] Being in this way, the struggle of the women should be directed in two directions to get "the destruction of the two main contradictions." That fight, therefore, would be articulated around two axes: around the class struggle and the liberation of women.

On the other hand, so many women supported only the feminist militancy, because in their opinion political parties and trade unions used the feminist fight for their interests, putting aside women's interests.[14] Even more, according to the independent feminists, being a member of more than one group made it difficult to make a decision and, at the same time, it did not guarantee to realize the systematic defense of the interests of the women confronting other opinions. Hence, above other options, they defended the priority of the feminist fight and just feminist militancy as valid strategy, in contrast to the other political groups. In our context Lanbroa was the paradigmatic example of this trend.

To a large extent, the approaches of those of this second trend, called independent, about the oppression of the woman coincided with the analyses done by the participants of the double militancy. The independents said that women suffered specific dependence and oppression as a result of their "feminine condition." In their opinion, that oppression materialized in one production mode that was not capitalist but that was in force along with it: in the patriarchal production mode, precisely. The fundamental unit of that system would be the patriarchal family, and the sexual division of labor materialized right there. That division assigned the woman the works associated with the reproduction work and family sphere. Thus, only women did those jobs and, therefore, they were the economic basis of the patriarchal system, the infrastructure. According to the members of this trend, the principal contradiction of the women would be the one that they had with the patriarchal system, which has been continuous throughout the history and has coexisted within the slave, feudal, or capitalist production mode that was in force in each moment.

Lanbroa combined this aforementioned radical discourse with a particular perspective of the difference feminism.[15] To articulate this conception of the category of *woman*, the "biological condition," along with the housework, was the basic element. It realized this operation through the emphasis of the differences among men and women. The women and the men, as a result of the different works done throughout the history, developed "specific characteristics" opposed among each other. In the case of the women, "tenderness, patience, affectivity, intuition, sensitivity, pacifism, the taste of beauty . . ." Men, in opposition, "aggressiveness, competitiveness, rationality, power. . . ."[16] Lanbroa's discourse, therefore, was characterized for recognizing some specific values to the feminine body. Lanbroa harshly criticized the feminists who defended the equality; it did not believe that the liberation of women would happen getting the equality, because it would mean to deny the supposed values of women and, at the same time, the assimilation of the interest of men for their part.[17] In this way, according to it, it was necessary to protect the aforementioned feminine values. They argued that only the positive reading of those supposed values attached to the feminine body would make possible the liberation of women. Thus, they defended the construction of a new world in which they could "develop all the affectivity, tenderness and sensitivity of women." Women were "the last redoubt of those values that the world needs."[18]

The trend of the feminism of the difference did not have a great development in the following years. Besides, by the end of 1970s, Lanbroa disappeared as a group but its members continued being members of the Assembly of Biscayan Women (ABW).[19] Lanbroa reappeared in the second half of the 1980s, as an autonomous group differentiated from ABW.

Therefore, the militants of the double militancy and the independent ones believed that all the women suffered specific oppression. The two trends confirmed that the cause of the oppression of the women was the sexual division of labor, which was based on the patriarchal system. But, while the first one asserted that there were two fundamental contradictions, based in class and in gender, the second one argued that the main contradiction of women was that which they maintained within the patriarchal system. On the other hand, the feminists of the difference argued that women are physically, emotionally, and rationally different to men and, unlike the feminists of equality, they believed that that difference needed to be preserved. But, this third trend was closely linked to the independent's perspective around the patriarchal oppression. They coincided in giving to gender an extraordinary importance in their political fight.

Thus, even if there were discursive and practical differences among the trends, all the trends which constituted the autonomous feminist movement emphasized the elements that united women, above those that differentiated them. Therefore, beyond those discussions around the organization, the political importance of the alignment among those trends needs to be underlined. In fact, beyond the mentioned difference, the discursive frameworks of those three trends built a strong political subject: the *woman*.

SEXUALITY AND LESBIANISM AS A DEBATE ISSUE OF THE FEMINIST MOVEMENT

In the 1970s sexuality was one of the main fight axes of the feminist movement. The feminists considered the current sexual model oppressive and claimed a free sexuality based on equality. Differentiating sexuality from reproduction, free and desired motherhood, and the legalization of contraceptives and abortion were the main claims of this stage. The free sexuality and the woman's right for pleasure and her body became a significant key of the slogan *the personal is political*. In this sense, the feminists' fight started in the agency of sexuality and body. The issues that had been considered intimate and corporal until then, thus, acquired a new political meaning.

On the other hand, sex orientation, that is, the subject of lesbianism, was also present in the debates of the feminist movement.[20] But, as we will see, the discursive framework that addressed it did not give it any strong political content to the identity category of *lesbian*.

Thus, the Homosexuality Group of the ABW introduced a paper in the mentioned conferences of Leioa that laid out two perspectives around lesbianism that, in their opinion, could have importance to design a future strategy. The former considered lesbianism as a sexual alternative among others, that is, as any other kind of affective and sexual relationship among individuals.[21] This perspective understood lesbianism as the personal and private option of each woman, denying it political content and, therefore, excluding it from the fight axes of the feminist movement. Anyhow, the authors of the text, in a vague way, were in favor of the second perspective. This suggested lesbianism as a strategy for the autonomy of woman and, in this sense, "in opposition to the heterosexual practice," it would be a means for the sexual independence of woman.[22]

Besides, according to these proposals, lesbianism, "simply, for being a relationship between women," would have some advantages that would exist "objectively," which would not exist in heterosexual relationships. Those benefits were associated with characteristics traditionally linked to women, for example, with tenderness, sensitivity, and imagination. And, at the same time, those relationships between women, "between two equal beings," would avoid the power of machismo and they would be exempted from violence.

But in a more important social and political field, and close to the approaches of the radical feminism in the United States,[23] the members of ABW suggested that lesbianism had a great capacity to destroy the patriarchal system in force. As capitalist and patriarchal society needed relationships among men and women to survive, women (like men) were conducted to heterosexual relationships. At the same time, lesbianism was considered an abnormal and aberrant practice and a deviation of natural inclinations. After all, according to the authors, that patriarchal narrative was an instrument to dominate woman and, in conclusion, the lesbianism challenged the patriarchal order. In any case, that approach did not have, at that moment. It would be addressed again in the 1980s but by the collectives of feminist lesbians.

Meanwhile, lesbianism continued being an internal subject among feminist activists. Outwardly, they protected lesbians, denouncing the discrimination they suffered for their sex orientation, but without putting this issue of the feminist's fight in the political agenda. In general, the discursive framework of the feminist movement idealized lesbianism, because it articulated it as a supreme practice, transforming and liberating in a wide sense. Considering the lesbian relationship a private option of each woman hindered to claim specific vindications about that issue. In this way, it contributed to the invisibility of lesbianism. Besides, in the first stage of the movement they prioritized the claims considered urgent, for example, the legalization of contraceptives, abortion, or divorce, and even the depenalization of adultery, precisely issues that only concerned heterosexual women. Finally, we must not forget that the feminist movement was not free from lesbophobia.[24]

After all, inside the feminist movement sexuality was also a fight axis. At the beginning, however, it did not have great influence in the identity of the women as a political category and did not become an oppression axis. As we will see later, the perspective to understand lesbianism would change in the following years, shaking in a deep and significant way the political subject of the movement.

LESBIANS AND THE HETEROPATRIARCHY

Lesbians mobilized in the feminist movement as well as in mixed groups, that is, in the movement in favor of homosexual rights. In that last option, in our context the Euskal Herriko Gai Askapen Mugimendua[25] (EHGAM), was the most significant mixed group. It was created in Bilbao at the beginning of 1977 and in the following year the groups were also constituted in the cities of Donostia (Gipuzkoa), Gasteiz (Araba) and Iruñea (Nafarroa). Despite being the minority in the mixed groups, lesbian collectives contributed significantly for naming their reality.

The lesbians gathered at EHGAM affirmed from the beginning that they suffered an oppression, and they spoke about their double exclusion, for being a woman and for being homosexual, which comparing with homosexual men, was an extreme exclusion. Society's ignorance of the existence of lesbianism would be one of the most significant features of that double exclusion.

This perspective changed with time as they started questioning the relationship among women. In 1979 many women of EHGAM of Biscay decided to constitute a group so that they could delve into the specific issue of lesbians. In that way it created ESAM, the first autonomous group of lesbians of the Basque Country. In this sense, the Basque context was pioneering, because, together with the Grup de Lesbianes of Barcelona per l'Alliberament Lesbiá,[26] ESAM was the only specific group in the State.[27] At first, although ESAM was linked to EHGAM, discussions around the organizational model rose from the first moment.[28] A short while after, they questioned the link among lesbians and gays and, finally they rejected it. It happened not only in the Basque Country, but also in the State.

Undoubtedly, the most significant component of the proposal made by ESAM was the ability to create a new reading of their reality, the one that joined with the political experiences of the feminisms of other countries. For the first time in the Basque context, the militants of this lesbian collective based their experience on oppression terms. In this way, in their words, the lesbians suffered a double oppression. On the one hand, gender oppression, because the lesbians, in so far as they were women, could be raped and the sexist and male chauvinistic legislation, the predominant morals, education . . . oppressed them and, in general all the things that meant exploitation and oppression for women.[29] On the other hand, they denounced that lesbians, for being a "sexual minority" suffered a specific oppression, that is to say, an oppression that heterosexual women did not suffer.[30] Thus, they were suggesting a new oppression axis in the feminist discourse, the differences among women emerging, which until then did not recognize them.

In so far as patriarchal oppression was the main element of the subordination, ESAM puts heterosexuality in the center of the analysis of the patriarchal system. Heterosexuality was the necessary condition of the patriarchal society, the imposed norm, the necessary axis for the realization of the sexual division of labor. In other words, the militants of the group were affirming that the patriarchal system needs "heterosexuals" and "monogamous" relationships "focused to the family" to ensure its existence.[31] Therefore, they considered that homosexuality questioned the patriarchal system itself, transforming it into a "potentially revolutionary political position,"[32] as long as the lesbian was conscious of it.[33]

In this way, ESAM renewed the theory about the patriarchy articulated by the feminist movement some years before, contributing to define what would later be called heteropatriarchy and anticipating the discursive framework of the collectives of the feminist lesbians in the 1980s. After all, ESAM's was expanding a new space, in which the homogeneous category of *woman* begun to weaken. Calling into question that identity, they radicalized and accelerated the denaturalization of (hetero)sexuality. This was seen inside a power relation, becoming a central element that emphasized the differences among women, turning into an oppression axis of some women only.

Thus, they were adding in the discourse new elements that emphasized the differences among women, differences that had not been politically significant until then. As we will see, that perspective would split, some years later, the political subject of feminism.

Since ESAM was created in 1979 and the First Basque Lesbian Meetings were celebrated in 1983, significant changes for the feminist movement as well as for lesbians happened.[34] Over the years, lesbianism stopped being considered as a private matter, a sexual expression among others, and became a space for the political fight. Besides, in those years they laid the foundations of the debates that would take place in the '80s. Even more, the unitary and strong vision of the political subject in force until then started weakening in the second half of the '80s. The lesbians would be (along with young women), as they opposed the straight feminist movement, the ones who challenged the normative identity of *woman*. The political subject, comparing with that of the '70s, would reword in a wide and diverse sense.

That new way of understanding sexuality suggested by ESAM had its echo in the First Meetings for the right to abortion held in Madrid in 1981. There, they declared that the strategy which should guide the fight in favor of the right to abortion must be based on the denial of the sexual models imposed by the patriarchy. The imposition of the heterosexual norm as the unique natural relationship made it impossible to differentiate sexuality from reproduction and, at the same time, it denied many women sexual pleasure.[35] Thus, for Silvia Gil these meetings "were a great step in the relation between lesbianism and feminism," among other things, because they admitted that "sexual relationships go beyond the heterosexual framework."[36]

In the first half of the '80s Basque lesbians increased the contacts among them and, as a result, in 1983 they celebrated the First Meetings of Lesbians of the Basque Country in Gipuzkoa. Although the main subject revolved around the organization, the collective of lesbian feminists of Madrid suggested that to get sexual liberation it was necessary to not obey the norms imposed by the patriarchy. So, heterosexuality should be denounced as norm. After all, to claim lesbianism was to question the patriarchal vision of sexuality.[37]

On the other hand, as mentioned, after discussing the organization models and the strategies in those meetings, the collectives of feminist lesbians were created here. Most militants came from the Women's Assemblies and, in that time, they decided to organize autonomously, continuing to associate closely with the feminist movement at all times. The distinction between the groups and the assembly sometimes was not very clear.[38] However, the collectives had to fight over and over so that the feminist movement assumed the discourse around lesbianism.[39] In this decade, the collective focused on the problems or subjects that affected especially lesbians, such as the specific assault and violence experienced by lesbians.

Even more, in the second half of the '80s, the members of the collectives discussed in depth the discursive framework addressed by ESAM. As seen, although the members of ESAM argued that lesbians were a sexual minority suffering a specific oppression, the discursive framework of the collectives extended that oppression to all women. According to the activists of the collectives, all women were subordinated to the heteropatriarchal norm, whatever their sexual orientation was. The heterosexual norm became one of the axes of the patriarchy, or, in other words, the heterosexual norm was the basis of the heteropatriarchal society.[40] According to this, "all women [are] heterosexual," "unless noted otherwise."[41] Thus, the patriarchy had two axes; the first, gender oppression and, the second, the oppression of the imposed sexual model. This new perspective would be able to unite and strengthen the subject of feminism and put it fighting against a "new" dimension of the oppression. But it was not that way. Despite that the heterosexual norm affected all women, the oppression level was different. It had "different forces and effects" according to the sexual practice of the individual had.[42]

In light of the above, the lesbians believed that their political practice should be aimed at destroying the heteropatriarchal society, and at denouncing the specific violence they suffered as a sexual minority. Thus, they denounced the physical (rapes, assaults) and symbolic (invisibility and exclusion) violence their bodies suffered.

The feminist discourse created the keys for the sexual liberation of women. But, that (supposed) universal discourse actually marginalized people who did not have heterosexual practices. The lesbians started seeing their sexuality not only as an issue that affected the personal area, it also affected the political field.[43] So, although at first (hetero)sexuality was not called into question and it was only discussed from the perspective of heterosexual women, the reflections around (hetero)sexuality afterward contributed to the formation of a new political figure: the lesbian. Lesbians' reappropriation and reformulation of the feminist discourse around sexuality caused the first crack in the feminist political subject. The lesbians declared that they were marked by gender and by sexuality, and that differentiated them from the rest of women. And that was the first fissure that contributed to give a new meaning to the category of *women*.

Women are Diverse

The Basque feminist movement that emerged in the Transition was immersed in a deep crisis in the first half of the '90s. Some militants foresaw that the end of the movement was close.[44] The groups, as the actions, had diminished.[45] Some feminists lamented that everything had been reduced to March 8.[46] At the same time, it seemed that the decrease in the ability to convene was the materialization of the weakness of the movement.

Coinciding with the decline of the movement, in the '90s, other categories of identity such as race, class and, especially, age and sexuality, acquired a major role, contributing to the rupture of the movement of the '70s and the unity of its political subject. The words of Tere Sáez about the Spanish Third Feminist Conference are significant:

"Those of us who attended were diverse and varied: young people, and women close to sixty. [...] Housewives, professionals, domestic employees, workers, unemployed, students, Christians, prostitutes, heterosexuals, transexuals, lesbians, physically handicapped, women from the academic world, gypsies, payas[47] ... As I said, diverse, the conferences with the most variety of women."[48]

Actually, this diversity was not new. In those conferences of 1994, as in the previous ones, many diverse women took part. What was different in the eyes of the feminists was that, until then, that diversity was not significant for doing the political reading of their reality. This explosion of diversity affected significantly the unity of the movement. But, even more, in those years the doubt around the political subject, the difficulties to define what being a woman meant, worried many militants. So many feminists announced the end of the political subject. Others, however, fought against the lack of certainty. And, in the center of this discussion there was a fundamental question: How would the feminist fight be able to survive without a unified and strong articulation of the political subject?

Conclusion

As Scott underlined, "There is no essence of womanhood (or of manhood) to provide a stable subject for our histories; there are only successive iterations of a word that doesn't have a fixed referent and so doesn't always mean the same thing."[49] The twenty years of the history of the Southern Basque Country's Feminist movement that has been examined constitutes an example of the idea of the American expert. In this case, the instability of the category of *woman* and its continuous rebuilding have been the axes of the analysis.

In the '70s, the solid category of woman and its body inherited by the feminists were so essentialized that they were not questioned. The trends that formed the autonomous movement, in spite of having ideological and thus, strategic differences, gave a new and revolutionary strong political meaning to the figure they inherited, constituting the political subject of the movement. The articulation of that new category of woman was capable of removing the differences among women and to emphasize the supposed elements they had in common.[50] After all, in the '70s, the category of woman of the feminist movement was articulated around the universal patriarchal oppression based on gender, and that is what gave it coherence and unity. As Butler points out, such operations are articulated "with certain legitimating and exclusionary aims"; at the same time, it naturalized the foundational fiction.[51] According to that American expert, the category of woman, constituted by feminist movements inserted in the identity politics, emerges excluding a part of the group that it supposedly represents.[52] However, as it is known, the normative discourses not only impose limits, but they also make it possible to create affirmative identities as well. In this sense, despite the fact that the normative, globalizing woman constructed by the feminist movement excluded other possible woman models, it enabled to the latter to restructure their subjectivity.

In the researched case, while the feminist movement strengthened itself, some members claimed that the movement was marginalizing some of its members. From the '80s, lesbian and young women were those who surfaced and denounced that exclusion. Besides the sexuality of heterosexual women, the feminists also dealt with the sexual or affective relationship among women. But they situated this second practice on the margins of of the political agenda, denying lesbianism its political character. As the feminist political subject emerged from a category based on homogeneity and universality, it could not recognize (or put it in the center) the specific issue of lesbians and, therefore, neither could accept it becoming a political subject. The stability of the subject was breaking in so far as its supposed universality was weakening, and also while they were building the new subjectivities crossed by many oppressions. The militants of the lesbian collectives, along with the groups of young women, built their identity unifying the different oppression axes in a summarily and hierarchized way but without questioning the feminine body.

In the middle of the '90s, the weakness of the political subject endangered the unity of the movement. In those years, the Marxist theoretical corpus, which in the beginning gave it a strong basis, had disappeared from the feminist discursive framework. But its weakness was not a consequence of a replacement of theories, but a change of the historical paradigm or moment. In that decade the feminist movement moved from one feminism of a modern or Enlightenment nature to a postmodern one. Thus, the rupture of Basque feminism was double; on the one hand, the breaking of the homogeneous political subject and, on the other hand, the prevalence of a new paradigm incompatible with the previous one. The success of today's feminist movement, among other things, is based on the deep reflection realized around those two axes.

BIBLIOGRAPHY

Aresti, Nerea, and Maialen Aranguren. "Women Above All: The Autonomous Basque Feminist Movement, 1973–1994", in *A New History of Iberian Feminisms*, edited by Silvia Bermúdez and Roberta Johnson, 328-335. Toronto: Toronto University Press, 2018.

Augustín Puerta, Mercedes. *Feminismo: identidad personal y lucha colectiva. Análisis del movimiento feminista español en los años 1975 a 1985.* Granada: Universidad de Granada, 2003.

Butler, Judith. *Gender Trouble. Feminism and the Subversion of Identity.* New York: Routledge, 1990.

Echols, Alice. *Daring to be bad. Radical Feminism in America 1967–1975.* Minneapolis: University of Minnesota Press, 1989.

Gil, Silvia. *Nuevos Feminismos. Sentidos comunes en la dispersión. Una historia de trayectorias y rupturas en el Estado español.* Madrid: Traficantes de Sueños, 2011.

Larrondo Ureta, Ainara. "La representación pública del movimiento de liberación de la mujer en la prensa diaria española (1975–1979)." *Historia Contemporánea*, 39 (2009): 627-655

Larumbe, María Ángeles. *Las que dijeron no. Palabra y acción del feminismo en la Transición.* Zaragoza: Prensas Universitarias de Zaragoza, 2004.

Llamas, Ricardo, and Fefa Vila. "Spain: passion for life. Una historia del movimiento de lesbianas y gays en el Estado español." In *ConCiencia de un Singular Deseo*, edited by Xosé M. Buxán Bran, 189-224. Barcelona: Editorial Laertes, 1997.

Nash, Mary. "Feminismos de la Transición: políticas identitarias, cultura política y disidencia cultural como resignificación de los valores de género." In *Entre dos orillas: las mujeres en la historia de España y América Latina*, edited by Pilar Pérez-Fuentes, 355-380. Barcelona: Icaria, 2012.

Osborne, Raquel. "Entre el rosa y el violeta. Lesbianismo, feminismo y movimiento gai: relato de unos amores difíciles." In *Lesbianas. Discursos y representaciones*, edited by Raquel Platero, 85-105. Barcelona: Melusina, 2008.

Pineda, Empar. "Mi pequeña historia sobre el lesbianismo organizado en el movimiento feminista de nuestro país." In *Lesbianas. Discursos y representaciones*, edited by Raquel Platero, 31-59. Barcelona: Melusina, 2008.

Puleo, Alicia. "Lo personal es político: el surgimiento del feminismo radical" in *Teoría feminista: de la Ilustración a la globalización. Del feminismo liberal a la posmodernidad*, edited by Celia Amorós and Ana de Miguel, 35-67. Madrid: Minerva Ediciones, 2007.

Rincón, Aintzane. *Representaciones de género en el cine español (1939–1982): figuras y fisuras.* Madrid: Centro de Estudios Políticos y Constitucionales, Universidade de Santiago de Compostela, 2014.

Scott, Joan W. "Gender: A Useful Category of Historical Analysis." *The American Historical Review 91*, no. 5 (December 1986): 1053-1075.

_____. "Gender: Still a Useful Category of Analysis?" *Diogenes 57*, no. 225 (February 2010): 7-14.

Zabala, Begoña. *Movimiento de mujeres. Mujeres en movimiento.* Tafalla: Txalaparta, 2008.

NOTES

1 * I want to thank Aintzane Rincón for reading and criticizing the text and Laura Cruz for her revision. It is part of the "La experiencia de la sociedad moderna en España: Emociones, relaciones de género y subjetividades (siglos XIX y XX)" project

(code: HAR2016-78223-C2-1-P (MINECO y FEDER) and the UPV/EHU Research Group "La experiencia de la sociedad moderna en España, 1870–1990, GIU17/37). In bold in the original.

2   The bold is mine. Euskal Herriko Mugimendu Feminista, "Greba feministaren hausnarketa, antolakuntza eta komunikaziorako dossierra," 7. https://grebafeminista.files. wordpress.com/2019/02/greba-feminista-2019-dossier2.pdf (consulted March 6, 2019).

3   Movement for the Sexual Liberation of Woman.

4   To have a broader view about the autonomous Basque Feminist Movement throughout the last decades of the twentieth century, see Nerea Aresti and Maialen Aranguren, "Women Above All: The Autonomous Basque Feminist Movement, 1973–1994," in *A New History of Iberian Feminisms*, edited by Silvia Bermúdez and Roberta Johnson (Toronto: Toronto University Press, 2018): 328-335.

5   Even though the legal possibilities of women extended in the '60s, the new power mechanisms strengthened the femininity based on love with husband and with children and, thus, many women denied those new horizons and connected voluntarily to that domesticity, see Aintzane Rincón, *Representaciones de género en el cine español (1939–1982): figuras y fisuras* (Madrid: Centro de Estudios Políticos y Constitucionales, Universidade de Santiago de Compostela, 2014): 179-230.

6   Mary Nash, "Feminismos de la Transición: políticas identitarias, cultura política y disidencia cultural como resignificación de los valores de género," in *Entre dos orillas: las mujeres en la historia de España y América Latina*, edited by Pilar Pérez-Fuentes (Barcelona: Icaria, 2012): 359; Begoña Zabala, *Movimiento de mujeres. Mujeres en movimiento* (Tafalla: Txalaparta, 2008): 27-28; María Ángeles Larumbe, *Las que dijeron no. Palabra y acción del feminismo en la Transición* (Zaragoza: Prensas Universitarias de Zaragoza, 2004): 69-70.

7   With "autonomous" I mean that assemblies organized themselves independently with respect to other political forces and institutions.

8   Unknown author, "Finalizaron las 'I Jornadas de la Mujer de Euskadi,'" Egin, December 13, 1977, 5.

9   Butler, *Gender Trouble. Feminism and the Subversion of Identity* (New York: Routledge, 1990):2-3.

10 Communist Movement of Euskadi, Maoist political party.

11 Mujeres del EMK de la Asamblea de Mujeres de Vizcaya, "Doble militancia," *Jornadas de la Mujer de Euskadi*, December 8-11, 1977, 67. Centro de Documentación de Mujeres Maite Albiz (CDEM). See http://www.emakumeak.org/web/

12 Unknown author, "Opresión de la mujer y doble militancia," *Jornadas de la Mujer de Euskadi*, December 8-11, 1977, 71. CDEM.

13 Mujeres del EMK de la Asamblea de Mujeres de Vizcaya, "Doble militancia," 67. CDEM.

14 Lanbroa, "Doble militancia," *Jornadas de la Mujer de Euskadi*, December 8-11. 1977, 62. CDEM.

15 The combination of ideas of different trends was not exclusive act of Lanbroa. In the United States, for example, keeping in mind the distance between both contexts, some part of radical feminism went to a more essentialist discourse, see Echols, *Daring to Be Bad. Radical Feminism in America 1967–1975*.

16 Lanbroa, "Valores," I *Jornadas de la Mujer de Euskadi*, December, 8-11, 1977, 59. CDEM.

17   Ibid.

18   Ibid., 60.

19   Mercedes Augustín Puerta, *Feminismo: identidad personal y lucha colectiva. Análisis del movimiento feminista español en los años 1975 a 1985* (Granada: Universidad de Granada, 2003): 135.

20   Unknown author, "Y qué pasa en los barrios," *Leihoa*, no. 1 (1978): 3. CDEM; Grupo de Homosexualidad de la Asamblea de Mujeres de Vizcaya, untitled, *Jornadas de la Mujer de Euskadi*, December 8-11, 1977, 15-16. CDEM.

21   Grupo de Homosexualidad de la Asamblea de Mujeres de Vizcaya, Untitled, 16.

22   Ibid.

23   Alicia Puleo, "Lo personal es político: el surgimiento del feminismo radical," in *Teoría feminista: de la Ilustración a la globalización. Del feminismo liberal a la posmodernidad*, edited by Celia Amorós and Ana de Miguel (Madrid: Minerva Ediciones, 2007): 35-67.

24   As many authors pointed out, at first feminists looked after the image of the movement, as well as the feminist (that already got bad press), and they made sure not to be identified as lesbian. See Raquel Osborne, "Entre el rosa y el violeta. Lesbianismo, feminismo y movimiento gai: relato de unos amores difíciles," in *Lesbianas. Discursos y representaciones*, edited by Raquel Platero (Barcelona: Melusina, 2008): 90; Empar Pineda, "Mi pequeña historia sobre el lesbianismo organizado en el movimiento feminista de nuestro país," in *Lesbianas. Discursos y representaciones*, edited by Raquel Platero (Barcelona: Melusina, 2008): 33; Ricardo Llamas and Fefa Vila, "Spain: passion for life. Una historia del movimiento de lesbianas y gays en el Estado español," in *ConCiencia de un Singular Deseo*, edited by Xosé M. Buxán Bran (Barcelona: Editorial Laertes, 1997): 202; Ainara Larrondo Ureta, "La representación pública del movimiento de liberación de la mujer en la prensa diaria española (1975–1979)," *Historia Contemporánea*, 39 (2009): 627-655. Years later, the Sexuality Committee of BEA would also recognize it, Comisión de Sexualidad BEA, "Algunos elementos de debate sobre lesbianism," 1. CDEM, Lesbianismo II/13.

25   Movement for the Liberation of Gays of the Basque Country.

26   Group of Lesbians from Barcelona for the Lesbians Liberalization.

27   Silvia Gil, Nuevos Feminismos. *Sentidos comunes en la dispersión. Una historia de trayectorias y rupturas en el Estado español* (Madrid: Traficantes de Sueños, 2011): 134.

28   ESAM, *Dossier Lesbianismo*, 1979, 26. CDEM.

29   Ibid.

30   Ibid.

31   Ibid., p. 18.

32   Ibid., p. 21.

33   Ibid., p. 26.

34   In these years, the feminist movement was submerged in the struggle for the legalization of abortion because of the well-known trials of the eleven women of Basauri (Biscay). That issue occupied many pages of feminist publications such as *Leihoa*. Simultaneously, during these four years an important impulse was given to the visibility of the lesbian question. The publication of a volume entitled *Dossier de Lesbianismo*, that I studied before, was a first step for this. Subsequently came the contacts with groups and people from the rest of the State and

the celebration of several meetings at the state level as well as the First Meeting of Lesbians of Euskadi in May 1983.

35 Unknown author, untitled, in *I Encuentros Feministas estatales por el derecho al aborto*, 1981, 21. CDEM.

36 Gil, *Nuevos feminismo*, 138.

37 Colectivo de Feministas Lesbianas de Madrid, "Heterosexualidad, lesbianismo y movimiento feminista," in *I Encuentro de Lesbianas de Euskadi*, 1983, 2.

38 Colectivo de Lesbianas Feministas de Bizkaia, "Esquema para la asamblea del 19.5.90. Lesbianismo," CDEM, Lesbianismo III/1.

39 Colectivo de Lesbianas Feministas de Gipuzkoa, "Componiéndonos las plumas," *II Jornadas de Lesbianas Feministas de Euskadi*, May 21-22, 1987, 3-5. CDEM.

40 Colectivo Lesbianas Feministas Gipuzkoa, "Componiéndonos las plumas," 4; Asamblea de Mujeres de Bizkaia, "Líneas para una charla sobre lesbianism," 1988, 3, CDEM, Lesbianismo III/6; Colectivo de Lesbianas Feministas de Bizkaia, "Algunos apuntes para una charla lesbianism," 1989-90, 3, CDEM, Lesbianismo III/5; Comisión de Sexualidad Asamblea de Mujeres de Bizkaia, "Algunos elementos de debate sobre lesbianism," 5-6. CDEM, Lesbianismo II/13.

41 Asamblea de Mujeres de Bizkaia, "Líneas para una charla sobre lesbianism," 1988. CDEM, Lesbianismo III/6.

42 Comisión de Sexualidad AMB, "Algunos elementos de debate sobre lesbianism," 7; Colectivo de Lesbianas Feministas [de Bizkaia], Comisión de Sexualidad [de la AMB], "Guion de debate para la asamblea sobre lesbianismo del 13-6-87," June 1987: 1, CDEM, Lesbianismo II/46.

43 Colectivo de Lesbianas Feministas de Bizkaia, "Una bofetadas en la cara del gusto público," *II Jornadas Lesbianas Feministas de Euskadi*, (Orio, May 1-3, 1987): 8. CDEM.

44 See, for example, Arantza Campos, "Eta orain zer?," *Geu Emakumeok, 19* (March 1994): 13.

45 Garbiñe Aizkorreta, untitled, *Geu Emakumeok, 20* (June 1994): 46.

46 Isabel Rodríguez y Andrea Bila, "Ahora te dejan entrar al WC, pero no bajarte las bragas," *Geu Emakumeok, 16* (March 1993): 42; Mariluz Esteban, "¿Qué es ser feminist," *Geu Emakumeok, 21* (Winter 1994): 32.

47 Non gypsy.

48 Tere Sáez, "Muchas y variadas," *Geu Emakumeok, 19* (March 1994): 12. As Tere Maldonado (ABW) pointed out, those meetings would be remembered as the meetings on the diversity among women and the plurality of feminism, Tere Maldonado, "Zorioneko Aniztasuna," *Geu Emakumeok, 20* (June 1994): 52.

49 Scott, "Gender: Still a Useful Category of Analysis?," 12.

50 Joan W. Scott, "Gender: A Useful Category of Historical Analysis," *The American Historical Review 91*, no. 5 (December 1986): 1063.

51 Butler, *Gender Trouble*, 2.

52 Ibid., 3-4, 13-14 and 142.

7

Tensions between Body and Soul: Homosexuality(s) in the Basque Country during the First Francoism

Abel Díaz[1,2]

Experiencia Moderna (University of the Basque Country, EHU)

INTRODUCTION

The Franco dictatorship's treatment of homosexual persons/behaviors challenges any linear historical vision of progressive secularization, of the gradual substitution of religious principles by physicians in the treatment of sexuality, as Michel Foucault had proposed. But, on the other hand, it demonstrates the validity of some of the interpretative keys developed in his works. The meanings around homosexuality varied in the normative imaginary of the dictatorship throughout the decades, and with them, the forms of social sanction. In the immediate post-war period, the reprobation of deviant sexual conduct was closely related to Catholic morality and, therefore, crime and sin were indissolubly linked. Later, in the 1950s, these visions were progressively influenced by medical evaluations, until a purely biological status was granted to non-regulatory sexuality. These transformations not only affected the treatment of homosexuality, but also its own ontology. Therefore, we will move from a justice centered on valuing the will and actions of subjects in relation to their sexuality, to another centered on the biological body as an expression of sexual deviance. What both conceptualizations of sexuality had in common was their intention to keep the sexual difference stable, setting the limits of what is acceptable for men and women. In this way, homosexuality represented an effeminate body/behavior, incompatible with masculinity. It is important to remember that Franco's justice focused its efforts on specifically punishing male sexual dissent.

Since its establishment, at the end of the Civil War (1939), the Franco government promoted the development of concrete laws for the condemnation of homosexuality and the imprisonment of the accused. These sanctions were based on the discourses of medicine, the church, or jurists, instances from which it was constructed as a deviant, sinful, and dangerous situation for society as a whole. These discourses should not necessarily be thought of as contradictory, if we take into account their interest in maintaining sexual order. The greater or lesser intervention of in the treatment of sexual deviance was a reflection of the tensions and changes in the meaning of the gender order at each moment. With this, we cannot presuppose that these were the only ways of shaping opinions or reactions to sexuality at the time, since we can also verify the existence of values proper to popular culture.

To conduct this analysis, I will focus on the judicial documentation produced by different administrative bodies in the Basque Country. In them, we will be able to appreciate a particularly representative sample of this historical evolution. We must bear in mind that some of the judicial administrations located in the Basque provinces attended, for these matters, a much wider territory, beyond the Basque Country. The administrations can well be considered as an expression of the treatment of homosexuality in the whole of the north of the peninsula, during the period.[3] The following pages will present a detailed analysis of the meanings of homosexuality reflected in this documentation, combining the sources derived from repressive groups or authors with other documentary typologies developed at the time. Advancing in the verification of the changes of meaning of the concept "homoxesuality", from early references to it as related to sin, toward others of biological nature in the 1950s. They will be related to the production of archetypes and gender norms of each moment, trying to qualify the survival and ruptures in the transition from one stage to the other. To this end, two judicial processes have been selected from the wide range of documentation available, which exemplify these two historical moments very well.

Homosexuality and its Historical Meanings

Studies on the treatment of homosexuality during the Franco regime are still incipient, and although we have a growing bibliography, many aspects remain to be explored. Studies to date have focused on the recovery of vital testimonies from people affected by the dictatorship, their experience of sexuality (from direct repression to various forms of silence), the study of laws against homosexuality, and, incipiently, the interpretation of judicial documentation, generally characterized by restrictions on access.[4]

For the Basque context we have an even more limited production and, in this sense, the judicial documentation explored in this work could be considered unpublished.[5]

Homosexuality, as a category of medical origin trying to give meaning to same-sex relationships, originated at the end of the nineteenth century in Western Europe. This new conception represented a radical change in the understanding and treatment of this reality. However, its introduction to the rest of society was always slow and irregular. Catholic discourses on sin that were already widely accepted acted as a brake. French philosopher Foucault defined this situation perfectly:

> Sodomy—that of ancient civil and canon rights—was a type of prohibited act; the author was but a legal subject. The nineteenth-century homosexual has become a character: a past, a history, and a childhood; a character, a way of life; also a morphology, with an indiscreet anatomy and perhaps mysterious physiology. Nothing that he is *in toto* escapes his sexuality.[6]

The *birth* of homosexuality represented a fundamental historical change in judging the sexuality of individuals, resulting in a process of essentialization of their bodies and practices. Homosexuality ceases to be something that is done, to be something that is. Although this biological condition was understood as an internal constitution to the anatomy, it ends up appropriating the whole body and appearing to the outside, being appreciable to any gaze. This transformation of sexuality did not operate instantaneously, but coexisted with previous visions, acquiring greater or lesser social influence depending on the context and the weight of the medical in the social order. It is important to emphasize that no understanding led to the absolute disappearance of the rest of the theories of sexuality, in evolutionary terms. Moreover, in many cases and contexts, they lived together and challenged each other, sometimes in absolute opposition and sometimes in various forms of confluence. Francoism is, in this sense, a paradigmatic example of these nonlinear and progressive processes in historical changes.[7] Medicine managed to reach a certain capacity of influence in the normative instances when we approach the 1920s and 1930s.[8] The victory of the Francoists in the Civil War represented a cut in this dynamic. The regime insistently rejected certain medical visions of sexuality, calling them leftist. In this new post-war context, some perceptions were recovered that affected the sinful nature of certain acts, put into practice through the judicial system and the crime called "public scandal", fundamentally. Without ceasing to represent a threat to the social order, a consideration that was maintained until the end of the regime, the meanings of homosexuality underwent intense transformations throughout the dictatorship. This study will focus on those that took place, in the so-called first Francoism,[9] although as we can intuit, changes and transformations in relation to sexuality and gender are always elusive to precise chronologies.

To interpret this type of transformation, this study will insist on the generation of different historical meanings of sexuality that shaped the practices of the repressive institutions of the State, the identities and ways of acting of individuals.[10] In a historical context where homosexuality was habitually severely punished, when it was perceived as an inversion or effeminacy, special attention will be paid to models of sexual difference and to the notion of sex as a historical construct.[11] In particular, the relationship between (male) homosexuality and normative masculinity will be addressed, to determine the extent to which the former affected subjects from the latter.[12] The meanings of homosexuality were directly linked to the meanings of being a man and historically evolved by questioning and reinforcing it.

THE RETURN OF SIN: SODOMY AND PUBLIC SCANDAL IN THE POST-WAR PERIOD

In the town of Tolosa (Gipuzkoa), at about "half past three in the afternoon of the twenty-fourth [. . .] of June," 1944, a man went to the Municipal Guard to denounce the events he had just witnessed. In his testimony, he stated that he had seen a soldier walking "towards the house where he lives," and suspecting the events that were going to take place, "he had entered the doorway in front of his house," to monitor the situation. From the place where he had hidden, he could see how the soldier and one of his neighbors "got into the doorway" of the building. The complainant, "looking in all directions, and when he realized that there was no one there, closed the door of the portal," because he feared that the two individuals had come to the place to commit "some abnormality." His suspicions were based on the fact that his neighbor "has a bad record for committing dishonest acts with men, and is known, in this sense, by the whole town." At that moment, he decided to enter the portal, surprising both in "a dishonest attitude, both face to face, and the soldier with his genitals exposed." As he witnessed the situation, he felt such "repugnance of the act" that "it made him put himself in a state of indignation" that "he began to distribute blows, and for that reason, he cannot specify if the [neighbor] was or was not with his organs exposed."[13] The authorities proceeded to arrest the denounced neighbor and opened a file with the Tolosa Examining Court. The soldier with whom he had had relations could not be located because he was outside the town.

The legislation at the time did not have specific laws for the punishment of homosexual practices and usually used the assumption of "public scandal" in the Penal Code. This type of crime had not been an invention of the Franco regime, as it had been applied uninterruptedly since the end of the nineteenth century. The authorities of the regime attributed it to renewed vigor incorporating it in its updating of the Penal Code of 1944.[14] The denounced neighbor was known for his sexual practices. In fact, in his statement during the trial he admitted to having been arrested and punished previously, having received, on at least two occasions, sanctions of 100 and 500 pesetas respectively. This prosecution is evidence of how the trials for public scandal, as in this case, increased in the heat of the legal reform. In historical terms, we are talking about a moment of transition from the most fascist stage of the regime to the most national Catholic model, which would prevail in the following decades.[15]

The first point of article 431 established the application of the crime of "public scandal" on persons "who in any way offend modesty or good customs with acts of grave scandal or transcendence." The ambiguity was present from the beginning in Franco's legislation. The law deposited in a third party the degree of offense in the consideration of sexual acts as subversive to morality. As in this case, the scandal did not emanate from the performance of sexual acts in the public space, but of the knowledge of the same, as in the jurisprudence appeared. The existence of this crime was understood: "even if they are not executed with publicity and if they had it when they were known." The crime would thus be determined by the "transcendence" reached.[16]

As is easy to guess in this context, those circumstances that could harm morals and good customs were directly related to attitudes contrary to the principles of Catholicism. Therefore, the homosexual practices of the individuals investigated here referred directly to the consummation of a sinful act. It is not surprising, then, that the statements that appeared in the process defined the situation as "sodomy." In fact, more medically-oriented expressions such as "homosexuality" were generally absent from this documentation during the immediate post-war period. It must be remembered here that, although in the medicine of the moment we find biologicist proposals closer to Foucault's notion of "character" homosexual, these had a limited capacity of action at the time of judging the sexuality.[17] It is representative of this period that figures as relevant as the psychiatrist Antonio Vallejo Nágera affirmed that the origin of the "perversions" was located in the original sin, committed by Adam and Eve. The psychiatrist even proposed a certain renunciation of the role of the doctor in the treatment of sexual deviations, affirming that the problem should be "endorsed" to the jurists.[18] After all, for the doctrine of the church, extramarital and nonreproductive sexuality always represented something totally unacceptable, and for this reason, a strong silence prevailed over it. The best option was not even to mention it.

Understanding the meaning of historical categories is always a complex task, because they are subject to a constant resignification process. The recovery of the notion of "sodomy" referred to this new political anxiety of imposing the values of Catholic morality. The difference between this understanding and another of a biological nature lay in the way in which the body was questioned about its actions. For the traditional doctrine of the Catholic Church, sodomy represented the rupture of the divine order (hence the *contra natura*), which was committed by the emission of seed in the sexual act avoiding the possibility of procreation. In this way, the mandate of divine creation was broken. Therefore, to determine the existence of this sinful condition, the authorities questioned each other about the acts committed by the individuals. Sodomy did not refer to a homosexual body, as an entity characterized in its deviation by its peculiar biology/psychology, but rather to a subject who decided to contravene the divine order by his will, which determined his guilt. Forensic medicine in the nineteenth century always understood sodomy as an act, in many cases making it coincide directly with penetration.[19]

The Instruction Court referred the case to the Provincial Court of San Sebastián, in charge of judging this type of crime, which could carry a prison sentence. The witness was questioned again, reiterating that he could not affirm that "the facts had been committed in their entirety." In the absence of reliable data on the events, the accused was questioned. The accused neighbor commented that he had had lunch with the soldier (whom he had known for about three months) and that they "drank abundantly" and then went to his home. The judge asked him to describe what kind of sexual actions had taken place, specifically, to which the neighbor replied that "as he was drunk he barely remembers, but he believes that neither of them ever got rid of his pants." Once the "accomplishment" of the act had not been confirmed, it still remained to be clarified which of the two had been the inducer, since the latter was more guilty. The defendant insisted on blaming the soldier for the proposed sexual relations.[20]

The homosexual practices of those investigated in this process clashed head-on with what was expected of a man from Catholic morality. Acceptable masculinity had to be characterized by its ability to control oneself, exercising a self-vigilance that kept him away from sin. In Catholic thought the human being is endowed with free will, and therefore, responsible for his actions. Sexuality was understood as the fruit of the will, and for this reason, its realization made it worthy of punishment. The fact of urging others to commit sodomy only intensified the breach of God's designs. The body, from this perspective, was constructed as a space of battle between the flesh, defined by its weakness in the face of temptations, and the soul, which directed the individual toward God. The moral person must have been "disgusted" by this type of sexual activity, as happened to the denouncer of this file. An assessment as subjective as that of the public scandal was measured through the physical reaction generated in the spectator, in this case the Catholic repulsion for unnatural sexuality. A very common expression at the time, to characterize homosexuality when it was illegitimate to speak of it, is to use the expression "filth" to refer to it, as happens in another judicial process.[21]

For Catholic discourse, the fall into sin was always prevented by self-control, and therefore noncompliance with the precepts could not be more than individual responsibility. Catholic doctrine harshly condemned the consumption of alcoholic beverages, as it led "to the brink of the abyss." In the judicial process analyzed, although Tolosa's neighbor tried to allege the consumption of alcohol as an excuse for his disorderly conduct, the authorities perceived it as another symptom of weakness. For these moments of fragility, the recommendation was always the same: "prostrate yourself before the tabernacle of the nearest Church." Although a double sexual morality had always prevailed for men, the normative accounts also insisted on male chastity before marriage. A manual published by Catholic Action recommended young men to remain "pure, pure, chaste," and to do so, they had to avoid bad company at all cost, and relate to individuals who had already "defiled his heart ignoble, as well as his body." [22] For that reason, young men should avoid, at all cost, any place with "bad fame," which could twist even the most upright conscience.

A body weak in the face of temptation, more easily permeable by the environment, was understood as being closer to the flesh and, by extension, to feminine nature. Here homosexuality was an effeminate behavior, not in terms of psychophysical deviation, but in the moral aspect. It was customary in the judicial documentation of the 1940s to use the term "effeminate"[23] to refer to the sexually dissident individual. The effeminate was the opposite of the post-war male archetype, represented by the monk-warrior, the ultimate expression of the insistence on the recatholization of men. Through these virile images it was a question of orienting men to the service of the highest values, to the rejection of any source of sin, going so far as to censor excessive interest in women.[24] The punishment of homosexuality was directly related to the maintenance of sexual difference, based on the ability to control sexual temptations.

The analyzed file was closed with a sentence that established as proven facts that the accused and a soldier had "given themselves to acts of sodomy." Acts that had consisted "at least in the exhibition by one of them of his genital organs." But mainly because the facts, "when known have produced the most serious scandal" in the "order of public morality." All this while acknowledging that their "publicity" had been limited. As such, the judge of the Provincial Court sentenced the neighbor of Tolosa to two months and one day of major arrest and a fine of 1,000 pesetas, in addition to the payment of procedural costs.[25] Thus, the homosexual acts of the accused were not only condemned, because they were dangerous for himself, but also because they were dangerous for society, as an example.

THE ANATOMICAL RECONSTRUCTION OF HOMOSEXUALITY IN THE 1950s

During the first Franco regime, the crime of "dishonest abuse" was used jointly with that of "public scandal" to prosecute situations that had to do with homosexual practices, often used interchangeably.[26] The assumption of abuse was generally used in the case of underage sexual acts. This was the case in a file opened on August 30, 1951, in Vitoria (Araba). A woman went to the police station to file a complaint against the doctor who had assisted her in her own home in January. On that occasion, the then ill complainant was accompanied by her nineteen-year-old son (still a minor, according to the legislation of the time).[27] After some time, the mother had discovered that, during this visit, the doctor had spent some time alone in the kitchen of her house with her son. Meanwhile, the doctor "pretending to want to obscure [*sic*] him and give him an examination," "unbuttoned the boy's pants" and then "started masturbating him until he expelled the sperm."[28] In this way, it was included in the file opened by the Court of Instruction of Vitoria for "dishonest abuse" of the accused.

To determine the consummation of the criminal conduct, the investigation focused on some elements of the defendant's conduct. During the interrogation, the defendant "categorically denied that he or she had or committed any dishonest act on the person of the accused." In the meantime, the young man confirmed what had happened, affirming that the doctor had done "ugly things with me." Everything was reduced to a disagreement between the parties, without being able to establish the facts as proven, since there were no more witnesses to the event. But the search for evidence progressively moved into the interior of the individual, and his body became the definitive proof of sexual inversion, as we shall see. The most definitive change with respect to the previous period was the participation of a forensic doctor who carefully examined the accused. The incorporation of this type of physician in processes related to sexuality was unprecedented in the judicial system of the dictatorship. From the 1950s onward, it will become a constant. Thus, the defendant was defined in the following terms:

> That from the result of recognition and observation, there are two foundations: in the first, a state of sexual aberration (paedophile homosexuality) is observed, which suffers from gift [...], influenced by the education received in the first stages of life and mainly at the time of puberty. Without appealing to complexes of a certain order, we know the influence that maternal support exerted on the examinee, many times we have known him accompanied by his mother when he went out to make professional visits. Raised and educated in this environment, there has not been developed

in him the just and exact conscience of the character and purpose of the sexual act.[29]

The category of homosexuality burst into this new context as an expression of the transformations taking place in judging same-sex relationships. It is not a simple change in terminology, it is a complex transformation of the meaning of these sexual practices. It was not the effect of a specific act to be determined, but of a condition present in the anatomy of individuals. The homosexual here constitutes a pathological state originated by an inadequate orientation. In this case, the forensic diagnoses carried out an exercise in body architecture,[30] of internment of medical taxonomies in the anatomy of the observed subjects. Neither psychiatry nor forensic medicine developed innovative investigations regarding sexuality during the first Franco regime. Their activity focused on the reworking of theories of the preceding decades. Here, the reference to pedophilia refers to the works of the French forensic doctor Tardieu, who classified homosexuals according to the position they occupied in the sexual act.[31] The insistence that the diagnosis makes on the mixture of constitutional and environmental factors, in the origin of sexual deviation, referred directly to the recovery of the theory of intersex states developed by Gregorio Marañón. The processing of this file would be characterized by a lack of definition or development, in the process of becoming an adult male, carrying in its anatomy and behaviors features of sexual indefinition, which approximated it to the infantile, and by extension to the feminine. Following Marañón, becoming definitive men or women was the result of a process of sexual maturation. Individuals contained in their anatomy the conditions to develop adequately, however, this process did not occur autonomously, and social vigilance was required to achieve this supposedly natural end.[32] In this case, the condescending role of the mother had contributed to the deviation of the son, within the misogynist imaginary of the time. In a manual on the care and education of children, mothers were informed that "desire is the driving force, which must be channeled" toward a "normal and healthy sexual life."[33] The coroner continued to assert:

[It should be noted] the psychic background of the personality of the explored, of shy and apocalyptic temperament, where the sexual constitutional factors have deformed the corporal sexual maturity."[34]

For medicine during Francoism, shyness in men was a psychic manifestation of their lack of sexual maturity, yet another evidence of the pathological proximity of the homosexual to the feminine. Sexually "normal" men had to show an "extrinsic aggressive" character, while femininity was characterized by "concentric and mediating" forms, in the words of psychiatrist Juan José López-Ibor.[35] The origin of the deviation of the defendant was not exclusively attributed to his progenitor, but it was recognized that it responded to a "constitutional factor," that is to say, that it was part of his nature. However, it was not absent of responsibility, since according to the forensic expert, "it has lacked attempts of orientation toward the normality of sexual inclinations; it does not even feel as pathological its current tendency." The arrival of the medicalization of homosexuality did not imply a decriminalization or deconsolidation of the accused. The presence of constitutional factors for sexual deviance did not determine the result of their actions, it was simply a condition against which it was necessary to fight. The individual will and the control of the environment continued to be central factors when estimating the guilt of the accused. Perhaps the medical theories recovered during the 1950s had a more decriminalizing character in the '20s and '30s. However, Franco's medicine elaborated a much more conservative version of these proposals,[36] whose sole purpose was to prove the guilt of the defendants. These changes, which were beginning to be observed in some judicial processes in the early 1950s, were reflected in precise legislation on sexual deviance. In 1954, an amendment was made to the 1933 Law on Vagrants and Malefactors, incorporating homosexuality as a specific crime, in the second point of the second article.[37] Here, deviant sexual practices acquired a more pronounced dimension as a threat to the social order. The direct result was a constant increase in the number of arrests and convictions for this singular condition. With regard to the Basque provinces analyzed, there was a general perception that cases of homosexuality had increased, as stated in the reports on public morality issued periodically by the Patronato de Protección a la Mujer (Women's Protection Board). This condition was "unknown" to the informants of Araba, Bizkaia, and Gipuzkoa throughout the 1940s, as opposed to the perception of authorities such as those of Gipuzkoa in 1952, which stated that cases of homosexuality were "increasing."[38] We cannot necessarily infer from these data a real increase in homosexual practices, but must rather interpret them as the result of a change in the way we question ourselves about homosexuality. What was in transformation was the authorities' perception of sexual deviance as a more dangerous situation for the sexual and social order in general. It is no coincidence that in these years one of the most openly anti-homosexual texts was published, *Sodomites* by Mauricio Carlavilla.[39] Previously in the background, changes were taking place in the conformation of a developmental society and the readaptation of the roles of men and women in this process.

Homosexuality also represented in this context a disorder related to men's loss of virility and their inadequacy in the gender order. A case opened by the Tribual de Vagos y Maleantes de Bilbao in 1957 defined as a crime the conduct of two men, who evidenced their condition through their:

> ... actions and gestures and on some occasions, during the night, conversations were heard [. . .] referring to "handsome men and ugly men," putting them in the same place that corresponds to women, although in no case has it been possible that among these repeated individuals the act of "pederastía" was committed [. . .].[40]

Sexual acts, which were central evidence in the sinful understanding of sexuality, began to progressively lose importance in judging homosexuality. Relevance was situated in anatomy as an expression of the disorder housed within the subject, which necessarily ended up taking over the body and behavior. Now, deviant sexual performances were nothing more than external demonstrations of an ontological condition against which it was necessary to fight. Thus, in the processes that were closed with a firm condemnation in the Court of Vagos and Maleantes of Bilbao, the forensic reports tended to state that this is an ontological condition against which it was necessary to fight "homosexual" because "their gestures and attitudes are characteristic of such individuals."[41] The way to avoid these deviant tendencies had changed in these years, and now marriage was understood as the definitive brake on male sexual disorder. A defendant in the Bilbao court was acquitted in the sentence because his "eagerness for complete regeneration which he will complete with his planned next marriage, which will undoubtedly be a great obstacle for him to avoid repeating those unnatural practices from which he voluntarily departed."[42]

The sexual difference was suffering a subtle modification between the masculinity referents developed during the Civil War and those more typical of a consumer society. The virile archetype of the monk-warrior, although it did not disappear from the dictatorship's normative discourses, began to lose its validity at the end of the 1940s. The male referent of the father of the family, as an expression of authority and order, was identified as a necessary destiny for the majority of males, not only as a personal duty but also as a patriotic obligation.[43] Therefore, the homosexual was intensely problematized by his failure to fulfill this "natural" duty. The effeminacy was in this context expression of various forms of inadequacy to masculinity, in an imaginary where biological nature shares space with the divine nature of individuals. In bodily terms, on the physical plane, it did not represent an adequate masculine image in the public space. A psychic shyness brings him closer to the feminine mentality, and therefore makes him incapable of exercising authority and sexual performance over women. Both, in addition, are understood as signs of intersexuality, that is to say, as a truncated development toward masculinity and, therefore, permanence in a childlike state. Here the homosexual was more a character than a sexual conduct, everything in him was an expression of his deviant sexuality. The operation consisted of invoking "less the enormity of the crime than the monstrosity of the criminal, his incorrigibility, and the safeguard of society."[44] The guilt of these subjects was in not correcting their condition, even recognizing their innate dimension, and therefore, not being suitable for marriage as the central institution for regulating relations between the sexes.

CONCLUSIONS

The Franco regime maintained a repressive attitude toward homosexuality through the judicial system, which was intensified in the Basque provinces. The condemnation of dissident sexual practices increased throughout the decades in contrast to what happened with repression of a political nature. This process was the result of transformations in the imaginary about sexuality between the 1940s and 1950s, changes that shaped the meanings of homosexuality and normative masculinity, realities that enunciated each other.

During the immediate post-war period, the condemnation of non-normative sexual practices was marked by the weight of Catholic ideas imposed by the victors. Although legal assumptions dating back to the nineteenth century were used in this post-war context, the effort was directed toward the identification of sinful conduct. The men were expected to be able to control themselves and avoid the sexual temptations that brought them closer to the carnal and the feminine. The arrival of the 1950s brought a progressive process of transition from meanings to theories of fundamentally medical origin. The biological acquired an increasing importance here, configuring the homosexual as a new character, affected in everything by his deviant nature. The men were judged for their sexual investment, but in this case, because it was considered a betrayal of human nature, which guided men and women to marriage and procreation. Both Catholic and medical discourses insisted on controlling the environments and will of individuals, and shared the gender order as the ultimate end, but not the procedures and meanings. It was not a question of substituting one model for the other, but of expressing tensions that were gradually resolved in favor of one form or another of understanding sexuality. Many medical and legal works continued to base their visions on the principles of the church and theology.

The increase in condemnations even responded to variations in the way sexuality was questioned. For Catholicism, sexuality itself was a gateway to sin, and it was therefore preferable to impose silence on these issues. Medicine, on the other hand, required a greater investigation and visibility of these phenomena at the time of establishing diagnoses and governing society. The result of these tensions was the creation of particular legislations, conditioning also their own forms of action and resistance of the processed individuals.

BIBLIOGRAPHY

Alcalde, Ángel. "El descanso del guerrero: la transformación de la masculinidad excombatiente franquista (1939–1965)," *Historia y Política*, 37 (2017), 177-208.

Alabarracín, Matilde. "Identidad(es)lésbica(s) en el primer franquismo," in *Mujeres bajo sospecha. Memoria y sexualidad 1930–1980*, edited by Raquel Osborne (Madrid: Fundamentos, 2012), 69-87.

Aresti, Nerea and Darina Martykánová. "Masculinidades, nación y civilización en la España contemporánea: Introducción," *Cuadernos de Historia Contemporánea*, 39 (2017), 11-17.

Aresti, Nerea. "The Battle to Define Spanish Manhood", in *Memory and Cultural History of the Spanish Civil War*, ed. Aurora Morcillo (Leiden-Boston: Brill, 2014).

———. "Masculinidad y nación en la España de los años 1920 y 1930," *Dossier des Mélanges de la Casa de Velázquez* 42:2 (2012), 55-72.

———. *Masculinidades en tela de juicio: hombres y género en el primer tercio del siglo XX*, (Madrid: Cátedra, 2010).

———. *Médicos, donjuanes y mujeres modernas: Los ideales de feminidad y masculinidad en el primer tercio del siglo XX* (Bilbao: Servicio Editorial Universidad del País Vasco/Euskal Herriko Unibertsitatea, 2001).

Arnalte, Arturo. Redada de violetas. la represión de los homosexuales durante el franquismo (Madrid: La Esfera de los libros, 2003).

Baidez, Nathan. Vagos, maleantes . . . y homosexuales. La represión a los homosexuales durante el franquismo (Barcelona: Malhivern, 2007).

Barrachina, Marie-Aline. "Discurso médico y modelos de género: Pequeña historia de una vuelta atrás," in *Mujeres y hombres en la España franquista: sociedad, economía, política, cultura, coord. Gloria Nielfa Cristóbal* (Madrid: Editorial Complutense, 2003), 67-94, 67-68.

Bernal, González. "La exploración en afrodisiología," *Revista de Medicina Legal*, 38-39 (1949), 167-175.

Blasco, Inmaculada. "Género y nación durante el franquismo," in *Imaginarios y representaciones de España durante el franquismo*, eds. Stéphane Michonneau, Xosé Núñez (Madrid: Casa de Velázquez 142, 2014), 49-71.

———. "Mujeres y nación: ser españolas en el siglo XX",Ser españoles en *el siglo XX, eds. Javier Moreno, Xosé Núñez* (Barcelona: RBA, 2013), 168-206.

Box, Zira. "Masculinidades en línea recta: A propósito del pensamiento binario del fascismo español," en ¿*La España invertebrada?* Masculinidad *y nación a comienzos del siglo XX*, eds. Nerea Aresti, Karin Peters, Julia Brühne (Barcelona-Granada: Comares, 2016), 223-238.

Butler, Judith. *Deshacer el género* (Barcelona, Buenos Aires, México, Paidós, 2010).

Cabrera, Miguel Ángel. *Historia, lenguaje y teoría de la sociedad* (Madrid: Cátedra, 2001).

Cleminson, Richard, Pura Fernández, and Francisco Vázquez. "The Social Significance of Homosexual Scandals in Spain in the Late Nineteenth Century," *Journal of the History of Sexuality* 23:3 (2014), 358-382.

Cleminson, Richard. "Instancias de la biopolítica en España, siglos XX y XXI", en *La administración de la vida. Estudios biopolíticos,* comp. Javier Ugarte Pérez (Barcelona: Anthropos, 2005), 127-152.

———. "La obra sexológica del Dr. Martín de Lucenay: entre el conocimiento científico y la recepción popular de la ciencia sexológica en *España a principios del siglo XX,"en La sexualidad en la España contemporánea (1800–1950),* edited by Jean-Louis Guereña (Cádiz: Universidad de Cádiz, 2011), 163-188.

———. "Marginados dentro de la marginación: prostitución masculina e historiografía de la sexualidad (España, 1880-1930)," in *Las figuras del desorden: heterodoxos, proscritos y marginados, coords.* Santiago Castillo, Pedro Oliver, (Madrid: Siglo XXI, 2006), 309-340.

Cuello, Eugenio. Código Penal. *Texto refundido de 1944 y Leyes Penales Especiales* (Madrid: Ministerio de Justicia y Consejo Superior de Investigaciones Científicas, 1946).

Díaz, Abel. "Los invertidos: homosexualidad(es) y género en el primer franquismo," *Cuadernos de Historia Contemporánea*, 41 (2019), 329-349.

Domingo, Victoriano. *Los homosexuales frente a la ley.* Los juristas opinan (Barcelona: Plaza & Janes, 1977).

Echalecu, Francisco Javier de. *Psicopatología* (Madrid: Publicaciones del Patronato de Protección a la Mujer, 1946), 265-267.

Febo, Guiliana di. "'Nuevo estado,' nacionalcatolicismo y género," in *Mujeres y hombres en la España franquista: sociedad, economía, política, cultura,* coord. Gloria Nielfa Cristóbal (Madrid: Editorial Complutense, 2003), 19-44.

———. "El "Monje Guerrero": identidad de género en los modelos franquistas durante la Guerra Civil," in *Las Mujeres y la guerra civil española, III Jornadas de Estudios Monográficos* (Salamanca: Ministerio de Asuntos Sociales e Instituto de la Mujer, 1991), 202-210.

Foucault, Michel. Historia de la sexualidad. Vol. 1. La voluntad del saber (Madrid: Siglo XXI, 1976), 56-57.

Freire, José Javier Díaz. "Cuerpo a cuerpo con el giro lingüístico," *Arenal, 14*:1 (2007), 5-29, 22-27.

Freire, José Javier Díaz. "Cuerpos en conflicto. La construcción de la identidad y la diferencia en el País Vasco a finales del siglo XIX," in *El desafío de la diferencia: representaciones culturales e identidades de género, raza y clase,* edited by Mary Nash, Diana Marre (Bilbao: Universidad del País Vasco/Euskal Herriko Unibertsitatea, 2003), 61-94.

Garza, Federico. Quemando mariposas. *Sodomía e imperio en Andalucía y México en los siglos XVI-XVII* (Barcelona, Laertes, 2002).

García, Francisco Vázquez and Richard Cleminson. *Los invisibles,* 5-8.

———. "El discurso médico y la invención del homosexual," *Asclepio* 53-2, (2001), 143-162.

———. "Políticas transgénicas y ciencias sociales: por un construccionismo bien temperado," *Seminario Teoría Queer: de la transgresión a la transformaciónsocial* (Centro de Estudios Andaluces, 2009): 3-14.

———. *"Sexo y Razón* (1997), diecisiete años después." *Cuadernos de Historia Contemporánea,* 40, (2018): 115-128. ID: "Homosexualidades. Presentación," Ayer 87, (2012), 13-21.

García, Francisco Vázquez and Richard Cleminson. "'Quien con niños se junta': la infancia y la iniciación homosexualista (1850–1936), en *Géneros externos/externos genéricos: La política cultural del discursopornográfico,* ed. Rafael Vélez(Cádiz: Universidad de Cádiz, 2006), 11-39.

———. Los invisibles. *Una historia de la homosexualidadmasculina en España, 1850–1939,* (Granada: Comares, 2011).

Gárcía, Mónica. "Sexualidad y armonía conyugal en la España franquista. Representaciones de género en manuales sexuales y conyugales publicados entre 1946 y 1968," *Ayer,* 105-1 (2017), 215-238.

Heredia, Iván. "Control y exclusión social: la Ley de Vagos y Maleantes en el primer franquismo," Universo de micromundos. VI Congreso de Historia Local de Aragón, 2009, 109-120.

Huard, Geoffroy. "Los 'invertidos' en Barcelona durante el franquismo y la construcción de la memoria gay. Un caso de cambio de sexo reconocido legalmente en 1977," *Feminidades y masculinidades en la historiografía de género, ed. Henar Gallego Franco,* (Granada: Comares, 2018), 213-222.

———. "Los homosexuales en Barcelona bajo el franquismo. Prostitución, clase social y visibilidad entre 1956 y 1980," en *Franquisme & Transició. Revista d'Història i de Cultura 4* (2016), 127-151. doi: http://dx.doi.org/10.7238/fit.v0i4.2442.

———. Los antisociales: Historia de la homosexualidad en Barcelona y París. 1945–1975 (Madrid: Marcial Pons, 2014).

Ibor, Juan José López. El misterio de la feminidad (Conferencia pronunciada el día 29 de

Septiembre de 1958 en el Teatro 'GUIMERÁ' de Santa Cruz de Tenerife, con el motivo de la inauguración de Aula de la Cultura), (Aula de Cultura de Tenerife, 1959).

Karl, Mauricio. *Sodomitas* (Madrid: Nos, 1956).

Krylova, Anna. "Gender Binary and the Limits of Poststructuralist Method," *Gender & History*, 28:2 (2016), 307-323.

Laqueur, Thomas. La construcción del sexo. Cuerpo y género desde los griegos hasta Freud (Madrid: Cátedra, 1994).

Lorenz, David Alegre. "Coser y desgarrar, conservar y arrojar": Visiones del enemigo y estrategias de supervivencia psíquica en la División Azul," *Cuadernos de Historia Contemporánea 2012*, 34, 119-144.

Mira, Alberto. *De Sodoma a Chueca. Una historia cultural de la homosexualidad en España en el siglo XX* (Barcelona-Madrid, Egales, 2007).

Mujika, Inmaculada, José Ignacio Sanchez, Iñigo Bilbao, and Amparo *Villar. Miradas atrevidas. Historias de vida y amor Lésbico y Gay durante el Franquismo y la Transición en Euskadi. Nuevos testimonios* (Diputación Foral de Bizkaia y Gobierno Vasco, 2015).

———. *Miradas atrevidas. Historias de vida y amor Lésbico y Gay durante el Franquismo y la Transición en Euskadi* (Diputación Foral de Bizkaia y Gobierno Vasco, 2014).

Nágera, Antonio Vallejo. Tratamiento de las enfermedades mentales (Valladolid: Santaren, 1940).

Olmeda, Fernando. *El látigo y la pluma: homosexuales en la España de Franco* (Madrid: Oberón, 2004).

Preciado, Beatriz. *Manifiesto contrasexual* (Barcelona: Anagrama, 2011).

Regueillet, Anne-Gaëlle. "Norma sexual y comportamiento cotidiano en los diez primeros años del franquismo (1939–1949): Noviazgo y sexualidad," in *La sexualidad en la España Contemporánea (1800–1950),* ed. Jean-Louis Guereña (Cádiz: Universidad de Cádiz, 2011), 229-245.

Rincón, Aintzane. *Representaciones de género en el cine español (1939–1982): figuras y fisuras* (Madrid: Centro de Estudios Políticos y Constitucionales, Universidad de Santiago de Compostela, 2014).

Rocamora, María Luisa. *La mujer, la madre y el niño* (Barcelona: Gasso, 1963)

Sánchez, Salvador Cayuela. "Por la grandeza de la patria: La biopolítica" in *la España de Franco (1939–1975),* (Madrid: Fondo de Cultura Económica de España, 2014).

Scott, Joan. "Género: ¿Todavía una categoría útil para el análisis?" *La manzana de la discordia, 6-1* (2011), 95-101.

Selles, Martínez. "Afrodisiología Médico-Legal," Revista de Medicina Legal, 50-51 (1950), 206-215.

Sosa, Miguel Ángel. *Viaje al centro de la infamia* (Las Palmas de Gran Canaria: Anroart, 2006).

Ugarte, Javier (ed.). Una discriminación universal: la homosexualidad bajo el franquismo y la transición (Madrid: Egales, 2008).

Ugarte, Javier. Las circunstancias obligan: Homoerotismo, identidad y resistencia (Barcelona-Madrid: Egales, 2011).

Vázquez, Francisco and Andrés Moreno Mengíbar. Sexo y razón. Una genealogía de la moral sexual en España (siglos XVI-XX), (Madrid: Akal, 1997): 13.

Vega, Aresio González de. *Para ti . . . soldado. Manual del Soldado* (Madrid: Ediciones de Acción Católica, 1957).

Vincent, Mary. "La masculinidad en la construcción del nacionalcatolicismo después de la

Guerra Civil," in *Feminidades y masculinidades en la historiografía de género*, ed. Henar Gallego Franco (Granada, Comares, 2018), 127-159.

———. "La reafirmación de la masculinidad en la cruzada franquista," *Cuadernos de Historia Contemporánea*, 28 (2006), 135-151.

NOTES

1 This paper is part of the Grupo de Investigación "La experiencia de la sociedad moderna en España 1870–1990," financed by the UPV/EHU (Código GIU08/15) and in the framework of the research project "La experiencia de la sociedad moderna en España: Emociones, relaciones de género y subjetividades (siglos XIX y XX)" (código: HAR2016-78223-C2-1-P), financed by the Ministry of Economy, Industry and Competitiveness and the European Social Fund, FEDER.

2 University of the Basque Country (UPV/EHU)
E-mail:abel.diaz@ehu.eus; abeldzdz@gmail.com
ORCID: 0000-0001-9966-3573

3 This study focuses mainly on documentation from the ordinary justice administration bodies in the provinces of Bizkaia, Araba, and Gipuzkoa (Provincial Courts). Also included in the study are the archives consulted from the Special Court for Vagos and Maleantes of San Sebastián and the Special Court for Vagos and Maleantes of Bilbao. The latter subsequently assumed jurisdiction of the Court of San Sebastián and also served the provinces of Bizkaia, Santander, Burgos, Araba, and Logroño.

4 Specific studies on homosexuality and Francoism: Abel Díaz, "Los invertidos: homosexualidad(es) y género en el primer franquismo," *Cuadernos de Historia Contemporánea*, 41 (2019), 329-349. Geoffroy Huard: "Los 'invertidos' en Barcelona durante el franquismo y la construcción de la memoria gay. Un caso de cambio de sexo reconocido legalmente en 1977," *Feminidades y masculinidades en la historiografía de género*, ed. Henar Gallego Franco, (Granada: Comares, 2018), 213- 222. ID: "Los homosexuales en Barcelona bajo el franquismo. Prostitución, clase social y visibilidad entre 1956 y 1980," en *Franquisme & Transició. Revista d'Història i de Cultura* 4 (2016), 127-151. doi: http://dx.doi.org/10.7238/fit.v0i4.2442. ID: *Los antisociales: Historia de la homosexualidad en Barcelona y París. 1945–1975* (Madrid, Marcial Pons, 2014). Javier Ugarte: *Las circunstancias obligan: Homoerotismo, identidad y resistencia* (Barcelona-Madrid: Egales, 2011). Ugarte:(ed.): *Una discriminación universal: la homosexualidad bajo el franquismo y la transición* (Madrid: Egales, 2008). Alberto Mira: *De Sodoma a Chueca: Una historia cultural de la homosexualidad en España en el siglo XX* (Barcelona-Madrid: Egales, 2007). Nathan Baidez: *Vagos, maleantes . . . y homosexuales. La represión a los homosexuales durante el franquismo* (Barcelona: Malhivern, 2007). Miguel Ángel Sosa: *Viaje al centro de la infamia* (Las Palmas de Gran Canaria: Anroart, 2006). Fernando Olmeda: *El látigo y la pluma: homosexuales en la España de Franco* (Madrid: Oberón, 2004). Arturo Arnalte: *Redada de violetas: la represión de los homosexuales durante el franquismo* (Madrid: La Esfera de los libros, 2003). *Para el estudio específico de las mujeres lesbianas bajo el franquismo:* Matilde Alabarracín: "Identidad(es)lésbica(s) in el primer franquismo," en *Mujeres bajo sospecha. Memoria y sexualidad 1930–1980*, ed. Raquel Osborne (Madrid: Fundamentos, 2012): 69-87.

5 In this sense, we have works focused on the recovery of testimonies: Inmaculada Mujika, José Ignacio Sanchez, Iñigo Bilbao, Amparo Villar: *Miradas atrevidas. Historias de vida y amor Lésbico y Gay durante el Franquismo y la Transición en Euskadi* (Diputación Foral de Bizkaia y Gobierno Vasco, 2014). ID: *Miradas atrevidas. Historias de vida y amor Lésbico y Gay durante el Franquismo y la Transición en Euskadi. Nuevos testimonios* (Diputación Foral de Bizkaia y Gobierno Vasco, 2015).

6 Foucault. *Historia de la sexualidad. Vol. 1. La voluntad del saber*, 56-57. García. "El discurso médico y la invención del homosexual," 143-162.

7 To follow the debates regarding the excessive dogmatism of some visions of Foucauldian theories: García. *"Sexo y Razón* (1997), diecisiete años después," *Cuadernos de Historia Contemporánea*, 115-128. ID: "Homosexualidades. Presentación," Ayer 87, (2012), 13-21.

8 Nerea Aresti: Masculinidades en tela de juicio: hombres y género en el primer tercio del siglo XX, (Madrid, Cátedra, 2010). García. Los invisibles. *Una historia de la homosexualidad masculina en España, 1850-1939* (Granada, Comares, 2011). García. "Quien con niños se junta": 11-39. Cleminson: "La obra sexológica del Dr. Martín de Lucenay": 163-188. Richard Cleminson: "Marginados dentro de la marginación: prostitución masculina e historiografía de la sexualidad (España, 1880-1930)": 309-340.

9 The first stage of Franco's regime (1936–1959) has been characterized by promoting a characteristic type of biopolitical system, which Cayuela calls totalitarian. Its main features are: a powerful repressive system, a situation of generalized misery, and subjectivities built around the *homo patiens*. Salvador Cayuela: *Por la grandeza de la patria: La biopolítica en la España de Franco (1939–1975)*, (Madrid: Fondo de Cultura Económica de España, 2014), 39 y 207.

10 As has been pointed out for some time, insistence on meanings has as its main precaution to avoid a "naturalized" compression of sexuality and to generate possible anachronisms, in: Vázquez. *Sexo y razón. Una genealogía de la moral sexual en España*, 13. García. *Los invisibles, 5-8.* Cabrera: *Historia, lenguaje y teoría de la sociedad*, 51-54. Aresti. *Masculinidades entela de juicio, 20-23.* García. "Políticas transgénicas y ciencias sociales: por un construccionismo bien temperado," 3-14. Para un mayor desarrollo de los debates historiográficos en torno al paradigma de la *incorporación*: Freire. "Cuerpo a cuerpo con el giro lingüístico," 5-29, 22- 27. Freire. "Cuerpos en conflicto. La construcción de la identidad y la diferencia en el País Vasco a finales del siglo XIX," 61-94, 66-70.

11 Scott. "Género: ¿Todavía una categoría útil para el análisis?" 95-101, 98. Laqueur. *La construcción del sexo. Cuerpo y género desde los griegos hasta Freud*, 33. Butler. *Deshacer el género*, 25. Krylova. "Gender Binary and the Limits of Poststructuralist Method," 307-323.

12 In this sense, the historian Inmaculada Blasco has pointed out as one of the significant changes of Francoism in terms of gender "that nationalism was involved in the design of a certain ideal of woman (and also of man), which gave a new imprint to the most traditional discourse on sexual difference," in Inmaculada Blasco: "Género y nación durante el franquismo," in *Imaginarios y representaciones de España durante el franquismo*, eds. Stéphane Michonneau, Xosé Núñez (Madrid, Casa de Velázquez 142, 2014), 49-71, 49. Inmaculada Blasco: "Mujeres y nación: ser españolas en el siglo XX," *Ser españoles en el siglo XX*, eds. Javier Moreno, Xosé Núñez (Barcelona, RBA,

2013), 168-206. Aresti. "Masculinidad y nación en la España de los años 1920 y 1930," 55-72. Aresti. "Masculinidades, nación y civilización en la España contemporánea: Introducción," 11-17.

13   27367, Provincial Court of San Sebastián (1944), Judicial Section, Historical Archive of Euskadi (Bilbao).

14   Domingo. *Los homosexuales frente a la ley. Los juristas opinan*, 24. Cleminson. "The Social Significance of Homosexual Scandals in Spain in the Late Nineteenth Century," 358-382

15   Catholicism and traditionalism were always among the founding principles of the dictatorship. Salvador Cayuela: Por la grandeza, 45.

16   Cuello. *Texto refundido de 1944 y Leyes Penales Especiales*, 384-385.

17   Echalecu. Psicopatología, 265-267.

18   Nágera: *Tratamiento de las enfermedades mentales*, 19-26.

19   García. *Los invisibles, 65-70*. García. *Sexo y razón, 16*. Garza. *Quemando mariposas. Sodomía e imperio en Andalucía y México en los siglos XVI-XVII, 79*.

20   27367, Provincial Court of San Sebastián (1944), Judicial Section, Historical Archive of Euskadi (Bilbao).

21   27711, Provincial Court of San Sebastián (1943), Judicial Section, Historical Archive of Euskadi (Bilbao).

22   Aresio González de Vega: Para ti . . . soldado. Manual del Soldado, 58, 60-62, 85-86.

23   27711, Provincial Court of San Sebastián (1943), Judicial Section, Historical Archive of Euskadi (Bilbao).

24   Aresti. "The Battle to Define Spanish Manhood," in *Memory and Cultural History of the Spanish Civil War*, 147-177. Rincón: *Representaciones de género en el cine español (1939–1982): figuras y fisuras*, 64-75. Febo. "Nuevo estado, nacionalcatolicismo y género," en *Mujeres y hombres en la España franquista: sociedad, economía, política, cultura, coord*, 19-44. Febo. "El "Monje Guerrero": identidad de género en los modelos franquistas durante la Guerra Civil," 202-210. Box. "Masculinidades en línea recta: A propósito del pensamiento binario del fascismo español," 223-238. Regueillet. "Norma sexual y comportamiento cotidiano en los diez primeros años del franquismo (1939–1949): Noviazgo y sexualidad," 229-245. Lorenz. "Coser y desgarrar, conservar y arrojar" *34*, 119-144.

25   27367 (1944) Provincial Court of San Sebastián (1943), Judicial Section, Historical Archive of Euskadi (Bilbao).

26   Cuello: Código Penal, 382-383.

27   Law of 13 December 1943 on the establishment of the age of majority. BOE 13/12/1943.

28   Documento 10032 (1951) Instruction Court of Vitoria, Judicial Section, Historical Archive of Euskadi.

29   Documento 10032 (1951) Instruction Court of Vitoria, Judicial Section, Historical Archive of Euskadi.

30   Preciado. *Manifiesto contrasexual*, 27.

31   Bernal. "La exploración en afrodisiología," 38-39 (1949): 167-175. Cleminson: "Instancias de la biopolítica en España, siglos XX y XXI," 127-152, 142-146.

32   Selles. "Afrodisiología Médico-Legal," 206-215. Aresti. Masculinidades en tela de

juicio . . . , 198. Aresti: *Médicos, donjuanes y mujeres modernas: Los ideales de feminidad y masculinidad en el primer tercio del siglo XX*, 120-130. García. *Los invisibles* . . . , 91-99.

33 Rocamora. *La mujer, la madre y el niño*, 51.

34 Documento 10032 (1951). Instruction Court of Vitoria, Judicial Section, Historical Archive of Euskadi.

35 Juan José López-Ibor: El misterio de la feminidad (Conferencia pronunciada el día 29 de Septiembre de 1958 en el Teatro "GUIMERÁ" de Santa Cruz de Tenerife, con el motivo de la inauguración de Aula de la Cultura), (Aula de Cultura de Tenerife, 1959), 25. Gárcia: "Sexualidad y armonía conyugal en la España franquista. Representaciones de género en manuales sexuales y conyugales publicados entre 1946 y 1968,"215-238, 223.

36 Barrachina. "Discurso médico y modelos de género: Pequeña historia de una vuelta atrás," 67-94, 67-68.

37 BOE, 17/071954. Iván Heredia: "Control y exclusión social: la Ley de Vagos y Maleantes en el primer franquismo," Universo de micromundos. VI Congreso de Historia Local de Aragón, 2009, 109-120.

38 La moralidad pública y su evolución. Memoria correspondiente bienio 1942-1943 (Madrid, Patronato de Protección a la Mujer, 1944), 77, 94 y 121. Año 1948. Patronato de Protección a la Mujer (Madrid, Ministerio de Justicia, 1948), 109, 125 y 148. Informe sobre la moralidad pública en España. Memoria correspondiente a los años 1942 y 1952, (Madrid, Patronato de Protección a la Mujer, 1954), 120, 139 y 170.

39 Karl: *Sodomitas* (Madrid, Nos, 1956).

40 Expediente n° 14 (1957), Special Court for Vagos and Maleantes of Bilbao (Provincial Historical Archive of Bizkaia).

41 Expediente n° 16 (1957), Special Court for Vagos and Maleantes of Bilbao (Provincial Historical Archive of Bizkaia).

42 Expediente n° 29 (1957), Special Court for Vagos and Maleantes of Bilbao (Provincial Historical Archive of Bizkaia).

43 Vincent. "La reafirmación de la masculinidad en la cruzada franquista," 135-151. Vincent. "La masculinidad en la construcción del nacionalcatolicismo después de la Guerra Civil," 127-159. Alcalde: "El descanso del guerrero: la transformación de la masculinidad excombatiente franquista (1939–1965)," 177-208.

44 Foucault. Historia de la sexualidad . . . , 167.

8

LGBTQI+ Lives in Basque Contemporary Novels

Ibon Egaña Etxeberria[1]

University of the Basque Country, EHU

This chapter's objective is to contribute to research into Basque LGBTQI+ issues from the perspective of cultural discourse and, specifically, contemporary Basque literature. Inevitably, several questions arise when we bring LGBTQI+ and literature together in the same binomial syntagma. Questions about whether gay literature and lesbian novels exist are not recent, nor are they wholly from the past. Many such concerns are derived from a modern, humanist conception of art in which literature cannot accept labels. Because of the that, rather than discussing whether LGBTQI+ or queer literature actually exists, it is more worthwhile to ask ourselves what we are talking about when we use that expression. Whether we are talking about literature aimed at LGBTQI+ people, literature written by LGBTQI+ people, texts which imagine non-heteropatriarchal lives, or a corpus of work brought together and interpreted from an LGBTQI+ perspective, for instance, there were almost no other works on this topic. I do not believe that the answer to that question can be the same in all cultural contexts.

In the Basque cultural context, literary production specifically aimed at LGBTQI+ readers was very rare, and until recently no lesbian or gay writers' community had existed in Basque literature. In the same way, there have been few proposals to re-read Basque literature from an LGBTQI+ point of view. So the aim of this chapter is to examine how Basque writers, whether identified as LGBTQI+ or not, have represented non-heteronormative lives in their literature, while being aware that such representations are not free from controversy, and that power-relationships and symbolic domination often cross minority cultural representations.

Basque literary criticism and research began to timidly move literary readings and interpretation of sexuality toward the center from the 1990s onward. Joseba Gabilondo started to examine Itxaro Borda's "lesbian self" in 2000 within the Hispanic Studies context of the US.[2] At the start of the new century, the subject in Basque literature began to be addressed at the few roundtable discussions, talks, and public events about Basque "LGBTQI+ literature" of which we are aware. In 2010 several Basque writers, critics, and researchers came together to write the book *Desira desordenatuak*[3] (Disordered desires), the only monograph about Basque literature written from a queer point of view. But since then there have been more publications about Basque literature from LGBTQI+ theoretical points of view. Transfeminism and queer theory were placed in the context of Basque culture, for instance, in the co-authored book *Genero ariketak*[4] (Exercises in gender). That led to several academic articles being published about Basque narrative and poetry based on an LGBTQI+ interpretation, and, in particular, articles about Itxaro Borda's literary production.[5]

My objective in this text is to examine how LGBTQI+ characters and lives have been represented in contemporary Basque novels, offering a path for looking at novels based, to a greater or lesser extent, on gay, lesbian or trans identity, and subjectivity. Not all novels which deal with LGBTQI+ issues have been taken into account, and this chapter's aim is not to offer a history or typology of Basque LGBTQI+ novels. I started to write this chapter with a more modest aim, and, with my own interpretation and intuition as my starting point and bearing in mind research conducted by several other researchers, these pages are designed to be notes toward a genealogy.

UNDER THE UMBRELLA OF THE NATION

Itxaro Borda published her short story "Klara eta biok" (Klara and me) in *Maiatz* magazine in 1986.[6] After it languished in press archives for several decades, when making an effort to bring lesbian genealogy in Basque literature back to life, Borda herself talked about it at a lecture in 2006 (Borda 2010). In 2017, she updated the text and recorded it to be used in Arantza Santesteban and Irati Gorostidi's short film *Euripean*. "Klara eta biok" is not the first Basque lesbian text, and Borda herself has mentioned several Sapphic poems by Amaia Lasa, as well as Arantxa Urretabizkaia's short story "Carmen." However, it does make sense to start our path with that narrative by Borda, not just because the coordinates which are going to guide her narrative are already in that text, but also because the conflict which was to affect Basque LGBTQI+ narrative in the 1980s and 1990s was also central to it—the tension between the nation and sexuality.

The main thread in Borda's narrative is Klara and her lover going around the streets of Baiona. The representation of the social and political atmosphere, along with the conversations and reflections between Klara and the narrator, are of greater importance than the events themselves. The story includes echoes from the political moment, marked by terrorist attacks by GAL (Grupos Antiterroristas de Liberación). The counterculture and punk movements also leave their mark. Outside official culture, on the periphery, are the two characters, with the chorus to Lou Reed's "Walk on the Wild Side" as their guide. From that starting point they reflect on relationships with men and on society, unable to find a place for their "mysticism."

Patriotism is a continuation of Catholicism, in the narrator's eyes. As far as gender and sexuality are concerned, and, to the extent to which she is fleeing from that system, the nation's protection is of no use to her when confronted by society. The two girls are "too cowardly," in the narrator's words, to be classified as heroines. The story defines the punk-influenced counterculture which Borda describes in the 1980s as something exterior to the nation, opposed to it. The narrative also offers criticism of identity control: in their conversations the two lovers criticize the police's "totalitarian" searches and, at the same time, their love is clandestine: in the eyes of the people, they live together just as friends. In this narration there is no affirmation of lesbian identity, but, rather, a desire hidden under the rain, in clandestine. Furthermore, Klara and the narrator also have relationships—purely physical relationships—with men, as do characters in Itxaro Borda's later novels.

After being published in 1990 for the first time, there have been more than thirty editions of Iñaki Mendiguren's novel *Haltzak badu bihotzik*, and it has become a real Basque bestseller.[7] At the center of the novel is the love between the nameless narrator and one of his students, a "heterodoxical love" between men, in the narrator's words. Mendiguren's work is set in a specific literary tradition (Isherwood's *A single man* comes to mind, for instance). The narrator being a literature teacher also provides the opportunity to make several literary references throughout the text (Forster,

Genet, Gide, Whitman . . .). The narrator expresses admiration for marginalized people, and the narration can also be positioned in terms of that affection.

The love between the teacher and the pupil is unnamed as the narrator's rhetorical questions make clear ("special friendship?," "standard falling in love?"). So sexual desire and relationships do not create identity in the novel. The two characters, in the same way, have relationships with women, although the relationship the student has with a girl and that which the lecturer has with a sex worker have a lot to do with revenge. Women are seen, to an extent, as objects for exchange, being used to project homosociality or jealousy between men. At the same time, in the discourse which the novel creates around homosexuality, the image of youths from Greco-Latin tradition exists as a literary trope, and homosexuality is seen as a hybrid between masculinity and femininity: "there is something strange in you, something between male and female," says the narrator to the student. There are also several literary tropes in the novel in connection with men's homosexuality: whether the student is looking for a father figure in his lecturer-lover; praise of the marginal; fleeing to the city.

Like a great literary tradition about male homosexuality, Mendiguren's novel, too, brings a tragic destiny to the relationship between the student and the lecturer. As the novel progresses, violence conditions and hinders the relationship between the two characters. Violence takes on many different forms in the novel: the student projects frustration derived from self-homophobia and aggressiveness toward the lecturer, for instance; but in the last part of the book violence is connected with the national conflict. Although it is not to be found in the first part of the novel, the armed-political Basque conflict shakes the thread of the narration in the second part when they give refuge in their home to two people who are fleeing from French and Spanish repression. That brings to them the "wolf" of the violence of the Spanish state, the ever-present threat, in the last part of the novel: the young man is forced to do his military service, and he dies in an accident during that time. The imposition of the Spanish nation and aggressive military masculinity bring violence to the young man's life, making his daily life impossible. So an equivalence between homophobia and national oppression is suggested in the novel, although Basque patriotism, too, is made responsible for homophobia. The tragic ending leads the narrator to proclaim the need for transcendence and to overthrow the system, proclaiming a homeland which makes space for heterodox love.

Laura Mintegi's novel *Nerea eta biok* was published four years later, and the lesbian love at its center is also placed in the framework of national struggle and political violence.[8] Here, too, a literature teacher and a student are the main characters. The central axis of the novel is the epistolary relationship between a literature lecturer at the University of the Basque Country (UPV/EHU) and a student in prison in Paris, and the main narrative voice is the lecturer-narrator's in the first person.

The correspondence-based relationship has no physical reality other than in the characters' imaginations, and the exchange between the two women is largely intellectual. Isabel, the lecturer, reflects with doubt and fear on the day when the prisoner will be freed, when their fragrance-less, touch-less relationship will take on a physical side. Isabel talks about a relationship she finds hard to put into words even though she does admit that she has fallen in love with a woman: "how would I say what I don't understand myself? Why can't I find the words to say what I want to?"[9] The narrator specifically refuses the label "lesbian," finding references from the literary tradition to do so: "What is being a lesbian? June Mansfield wasn't a lesbian, nor was Anais Nin, and they loved each other, with fiery desire, and they both loved Henry Miller."[10] The narrator keeps her relationship with Nerea quiet and, so, the love between the two women has no name and does not exist as far as other people are concerned, and Nerea often fulfills the role of the writer's conscience rather than being a flesh-and-blood character.

The intellectual complicity between the two women is the basis for the relationship (they are both literature fans, both committed to their nation), and love for a nation and love for a person are often compared, being shown as the basis on which they are able to stay alive. However, the narrator does not reject love for men and, in fact, her relationship with Nerea is a space for her to talk about and discuss relationships with men: "What do you want 'our' man to be like? What's your type?"[11] The relationship she has with her student, to that extent, is a framework for reflecting on love for men now and in the past, and on motherhood.

Motherhood, in fact, moves to the center of the narrator's subjectivity toward the end of the novel, and she moves away from intellectuality back to corporality, and to stopping her relationship with Nerea too. After Nerea leaves prison, when their Platonic love could have taken on a physical side, it does not, and, a few months later, when they arrest and imprison Isabel's son, her motherhood comes to the fore in a political sense. The narrator decides to take on the role of protector and defender of her imprisoned son, offering her life to that cause, and what had been her intellectual relationship with prison becomes a real, physical relationship in that way. So when the national conflict breaks out within the family, love for a woman with no future or transcendence becomes something of the past. "If it's between women it is, in general, something temporary, without consequences, or any history, it only exists in the present,"[12] says the narrator at one moment; on the other hand, love for the nation—which combines taking care of her son and being involved in the political struggle—gives the lecturer a utopian projection toward the future. So at the end of the novel the gender-logic of nationalism prevails, and the nation's reproductive function prevails over lesbian desire.[13]

Karlos Gorrindo wrote his novel *Ni naizen hori* when he was in prison; the narration brings national conflict and gender-identity together.[14] The novel—published in 1992—follows two characters' movements from the start and until their destinies cross at the end. Mario is the first of the two, who works in a bookshop in Bilbao; Kepa is the second, a young Euskadi Ta Askatasuna (ETA) activist. After meeting a "transvestite" called Afrika, Mario finds the mirror necessary to affirm her identity: "Afrika, I identify with your way of being completely; I, too, feel what I haven't been. I feel I'm a woman inside a man's body."[15] Mario/Marilin constructs her transgender personality based on the rhetoric of a person born in the wrong body and on mistaken nature. She refuses categories such as "homosexual" and "transvestite" and proclaims her womanhood, being a "man" from the outside only, her essence being that of women. Mario faces the roughest conflicts when she starts to socialize as a woman and with the name Marilin, her relationship with her parents is broken, she becomes unemployed . . .

As in many Basque novels, a specific chronotope is formed by the Bilbao district of San Frantzisko during the 1980s and 1990s, in which marginalized people, clandestinity, and resistance come together. Afrika introduces Mario to that nighttime atmosphere, and it is in those surroundings that she meets ETA activist Kepa. Meeting him is the keystone to constructing her identity, and also to the development of the story. The novel suggests equivalence between groups of people and subjective perspectives which live on the edges of the law, specifically between transgender groups and members of ETA, which is made possible by the novel's chronotope. During her night encounter with Kepa, Marilin receives recognition for her identity from the activist, something nobody else has given her: "for me, you're a woman."[16] In the strongly symbolic ending, on the other hand, Kepa, wounded, takes refuge in Marilin's apartment after a shoot-out with the police, and the love between the two characters gives the story a happy ending. The character's gender-transition reaches its conclusion when she takes on the role of the ETA activist's nurse and carer. To put it another way, Marilin is recognized as a woman by reproducing the gender roles of nationalism, when she takes on the role of the soldier's carer.

The national struggle is a conflict which brings other factors together in Gorrindo's novel. The graphic representation of that appears when Mario comes across a demonstration in Bilbao in which, under the slogan "We are a Nation," several different proclamations come together: feminists, demands for sexual freedom, people demanding an amnesty for Basque prisoners . . . So it is the nation which brings all the other conflicts and demands together, including that for sexual freedom. Helena González used the expression "totalizing umbrella" to explain how in certain cultural areas—in Galicia, for instance—discourse about the nation covers up and simplifies other conflicts and tensions including those connected with gender.[17] In these 1990s novels, too, the discourse of nation and other tensions connected with it put the other conflicts into a framework either by preventing homosexual desire by using political violence, or by reapplying the heterosexual regime's roles and norms on LGTB characters' lives.

No Nation? Connemara, London, Manchester

During the 1990s Basque narrative was taken by the need to represent reality, and a sort of anxiety for realist novels arose in the literature.[18] When wanting to depict reality, representing sociopolitical reality and the political-armed conflict became particularly necessary. It is in that context that the space which Mintegi, Gorrindo, and Mendiguren's novels give to the national conflict should be understood. The few narratives which had homosexual desire at their center and which were able to avoid tragedies from occurring had no intention of representing sociopolitical reality. They were written and published at the margins of canonical literature, some of them brought out in paraliterary circles. Aitor Arana's work deserves a special mention in that area, editing the erotic gay literary magazine *Xut* from 1992 to 1996, a fanzine-type underground magazine supported by EHGAM. In addition to that, Arana's novels *Aita-semeak* (1995) and *Onan* (2000)[19] were free from conventional realist depictions, among other things, and made space for homosexual pleasure and desire without taking many taboos into account (incest and so on).

At the same time, social discourses about sexuality were changing, unquestionably, and ideas about normalization were of increasing importance in the literary field too. Iñigo Lamarca's *Gay nauzu*[20] (I'm gay, 1999) was an autobiographical book about events he witnessed in connection with his homosexual experiences. Starting in his adolescence, his biography concludes with him leading a normalized adult gay life and proclaiming equality. Lamarca's discourse is indicative of the strengthening of normalization in the cultural and sociopolitical areas during the 2000s, and the text may be seen as symptomatic of that. Influenced by changes which had taken place in the framework around society and sexuality, the number of gay and lesbian characters increased in Basque novels. Gay characters, however, were often isolated second-level figures in novels, living in wholly heterosexual environments and inevitably condemned to solitude.[21] In other cases, though, writers sought out elements of surprise using mysteries that uncovered homosexuality in noire-type narratives, among others.[22]

In any case, during the 2000s the totalizing umbrella of the nation continued to mark the coordinates, and it is no surprise that the gay and lesbian characters and relationships in novels are set abroad, although fleeing abroad does not always involve fleeing from the nation and its framework. Julen Gabiria's successful *Connemara gure bihotzetan*[23] (Connemara in our hearts, 2000) is set in the Basque Country and Ireland, and the hidden secret it reveals is one of the character's lesbian relationship. After lead character Txema's girlfriend dies in a road accident, he goes on the same trip around Ireland that she had taken a year earlier. As he reads Eider's diary, he finds out, among other things, about her romance with a girl named Rocio from California. Her boyfriend reads that she had felt dead in the Basque Country and only found the path for her desire in Ireland, having love stories with both Rocio and Ralph, for instance. Being abroad makes it possible to come across other people (Rocio's otherness is represented by her "looking Andalusian"). But the foreign land in the novel is essentially a mirror for the Basque Country: Eider becomes fascinated with Ireland after an IRA attack, and the ending of the novel does not escape from the national conflict's framework or from the traditional female role. Although she does not play an active role in the Irish conflict, Eider's relationships with men do involve her, and her tragic death brings the false freedom she had experienced to the fore along with that character's impossibility to live.

Nationality and gay identity are among the most complex issues in Juanjo Olasagarre's *Ezinezko maletak*[24] (Impossible suitcases, 2004). Two confrontations between space and time are represented: London of 2000 and a small town in Navarre in the 1980s. This novel's present day is centered on a dead character: Carlos Bazterretxea "Bazter" has just died in London when the narrative starts. The friends of his youth go to his funeral, and the book goes backward and forward in time along with the journey, comparing Bazter and his friends' past and present. The narrative jumps between the two chronotopes: a small Basque-speaking, patriotic town in Navarre in the 1980s in which the young people—including Bazter and his friends—are committed to the struggle for national freedom; and London, on the other hand, where Bazter redefines himself as gay and forms his own "family" with his boyfriend, lovers, and several other friends.

The novel's foundational moment is when Bazter decides to leave his town and go abroad. He decides to leave the Basque Country as the promises based on revolution and the nation—that sexuality will become liberated at the same time as the nation, for instance—do not enable him to live out his sexuality. In addition to a change of place this brings the character a change of identity and, unlike in previous Basque novels, Olasagarre's character proclaims his gayness. Going beyond sexual practice and desire, Bazter being gay is also an identity, and that statement clashes with his being Basque. As he lives in London he is "no longer a Basque" he confesses to Mark, his boyfriend. Denying being Basque opens the way for the lead character to live a gay life and, to that extent, to avoid the destiny faced by most gay characters in novels until then: a tragic, isolated destiny.

Rather than just relating how Basque nationality replaces gay identity, *Ezinezko maletak* is a novel that asks questions about changeability. The friends who go to Bazter's funeral in London take a Basque flag to put on his coffin; his transvestite friend Ike, on the other hand, takes the rainbow flag. The "war" between the two flags and the discussions between the characters at the funeral compare two points of view: Harakin, a friend from his youth, says that Bazter had "always been Basque," while Ike says he had been "from the queer world." Although he wants to reject his nationality, Bazter does not completely manage to develop a genuine project around his gayness, and the novel suggests that he cannot completely flee from his hegemonic national identity. Which is why the novel offers the opportunity for parody, hyperbole, and farce as a way out, particularly through the character Ike.

Irati Jimenez published *Bat, bi, Manchester*[25] two years later, telling the story of two young Basque men who lived in that English city in the 2000s. The characters' Basqueness is not a source of conflict, there being no mention of the national conflict in Jimenez's story. In fact, the narrator and main character puts Manchester and Bilbao on the same level, and there is no confrontation between the two places; so the narration shows them as examples of the removal of differences in post-modern, globalized times. So it might be thought that placing the two characters abroad was deliberate to avoid the national conflict, placing them outside the national umbrella. Conflict, then, is of another kind in the narrative: impossible romantic love puts the lead character in tension as he falls in love with his heterosexual flatmate, and that unsatisfied desire is a source of frustration: "unwritten novels and heterosexuals we will never have. They are endless sources of frustration."[26] Identity is not a source of conflict and, likewise, desire does not lead the character to proclaim a gay identity; perhaps that is why impossible romantic love and isolation are his destiny. To an extent this novel can be set in the context of the "normalisation" of gayness and globalisation of the 2000s. But, at the same time, the lack of statement of gay identity and the lack of an LGTB community bring that limited path to normalization to light.

LESBIAN REINVENTIONS

Itxaro Borda's literary path has been that taken by the detective Amaia Ezpeldoi since the 1990s, and it is impossible to address lesbian Basque narrative without examining Ezpeldoi's career. *Bakean ützi arte*[27] (Until left alone, 1994) was leading character Ezpeldoi's first novel, and in 1996 she was the main figure in two more novels, *Amorezko pena bañ o*[28] (Rather than lovesick) and *Bizi nizano munduan* (While I live in the world).[29] In these three novels the investigations which rural detective Ezpeldoi conducts give Borda the opportunity to examine several social conflicts, and in each she develops several social critiques (environmentalism, militarism, family critique . . .).[30] Borda places her characters in a rural, peripheral Basque Country, writing the novels in peripheral, non-hegemonic Basque dialects. In those peripheral geographical and linguistic settings, Borda represents a hybrid Basque Country which confronts hegemonic nationalism from the periphery.[31]

In those novels Borda's characters were "mute." As the author has sometimes stated (2010), they did not dare to say "what" they were. In other words, they did not accept their own lesbian identity, and, in spite of desiring women, they also had relationships with men. After a decade without any new Ezpeldoi novels, in 2007 *Jalgi hadi plazara*[32] (Come out in public) was published, and this story brought changes with it. While using the same coordinates as in the previous Amaia Ezpeldoi books, statements of identity bring changes to the character's development. In this parodic detective novel a member of the Academy of the Basque Language's disappearance and kidnapping has to be cleared up, and this provides the pretext for a type of road movie around many places in the Basque Country, from the northern Basque Country to Gasteiz, and finally, on to Bilbao. But the Bilbao of the 2000s is not the city in decline represented by Basque narrative in the 1990s, but, rather, a global, cosmopolitan city, transformed by the Guggenheim effect. The route starts in the northern Basque Country and finishes in Bilbao, so Amaia Ezpeldoi goes from a rural, peripheral setting to the center. In the city she finds the place to state her identity, and it is the first time she defines herself to herself and to others as "lesbian." It is a foundational moment for Ezpeldoi, as her lover Carmen tells her: "at the moment you recognise it, even if only half way, your life makes a lot of sense (. . .) At the instant you recognise it you can regret having taken part in a game which isn't on your playing field."[33] That performative naming also opens the way for Ezpeldoi to leave her melancholy behind.

However, the statement of Ezpeldoi's lesbian identity cannot be understood without questioning and reformulating her attitude to the Basque nation. For one thing, at the start of the novel the character mentions that she had left her communist ideology behind her when she moved from Maule to Baiona, and her patriotism too, although she says that she had never been a fervent patriot: "after a certain time I had no political opinions because I had spent so long fiercely defending my own ideas."[34] So it can be understood that Ezpeldoi's lesbianism is proclaimed after she leaves her patriotism behind her and moves away from ideologies. But that does not lead to a complete distancing from the Basque nation and Basque culture; the new identity which Ezpeldoi proposes connects the Basque language and being a lesbian, and that is how the novel's title, too, must be understood, "Jalgi hadi" being a pro-Basque reference as well as being in favor of coming out. The two ideas are specifically linked at the end of the novel, Basque and lesbianism being brought together in a single word: "I was trapped in love and my heart said to me: come out in public ("Jalgi hadi plazara"), Basque, lesbian, Basque, lesbian, eusleskarabianakaralesbeusbianaka."[35]

The book, set during ETA's ceasefire, also parodies the armed conflict to an extent, bringing a former member of ETA, a police officer, and a transsexual singer together with Amaia Ezpeldoi on the road movie. Borda puts forward a post-conflict type of nationality through Ezpeldoi, once more taking the periphery as her thread: Transgender singer Haizemin, who sings in the Zuberoa dialect in Bilbao, can be seen as a metaphor for a Basque-speaking, non-nationalist, queer utopian Basque Country.

After proclaiming herself to be a lesbian in the novel *Jalgi hadi plazara*, in the following work Amaia Ezpeldoi continues to state her identity, and also imagines a Basque lesbian and LGBTQI+ community. In the novel *Boga boga*[36] (2012) Ezpeldoi and lesbians from many different places get together at a bar called Wittig in Biarritz. Referencing Monique Wittig and placing her in the center, in this novel Borda puts together her own lesbian reference world, and the solitary Ezpeldoi finds herself in the heart of a lesbian community. Although nationality and the political-armed conflict are also present in this novel, it is worth underlining that the conflict is already portrayed as something from the past. Ezpeldoi investigates several unsolved murders from the 1980s, and, to do so, has to return to the situation of the northern Basque Country in 1985, the atmosphere represented in *Klara eta biok*. So the national conflict is moved to the area of memory and narration in Ezpeldoi's investigations.

Borda's novel puts forward an idea for reinventing Basque lesbianism; several novels by a younger generation, on the other hand, have represented lesbianism itself as a utopian, political way to reinvent characters and subjects and free them from their ties. In Uxue Apaolaza's novel *Mea culpa*[37] (2011), lesbianism is a way to escape from the patriarchy, heterosexual norms, and the national conflict. Lur, a 30-year-old woman, is the main character: born in an unnamed town in the Basque Country, she has been living in Madrid for several years, the political activism and friendships of her youth forgotten. When one of the friends of her youth, Mikel, is arrested under the accusation of being a member of ETA, Lur suddenly wants to get away from everything, and she drives away to Les Landes. For no apparent reason, she decides to kill some of the friends of her youth who are there on holiday, one by one. In an endless digression, Lur remembers her youth in the 1990s in the unnamed town, which she had spent in a community formed around the Basque Left, and the guilt she feels because of ETA's murders sharpens her hunger for revenge.

Although she is isolated in Les Landes, Lur does become friends with a neighbor, and in that neighbor she finds a mirror for reconstructing herself. Elisa, a woman who has stopped looking after her family's well-being in her old age, is a character who has proclaimed herself to be a lesbian and knows how to enjoy herself; she is learning to live outside heterosexual norms and, to an extent, she is also a projection of the main character's desires. The 70-year-old woman has achieved what Lur has not: freeing herself from the trauma created by the national conflict, and fleeing from the traditional role imposed on her by the heterosexual context of the armed conflict. Lesbianism is her way to reinvent the subjectivity, which is embodied in the utopic, idealized character Elisa, who can be taken as Lur's projection or fantasy.

In Danele Sarriugarte's novel *Azala erre*[38] (Burn skin, 2018), too, lesbianism is represented as a way to escape from the patriarchy, masculine abuse of power, and symbolic violence, and a way to reinvent identity. The novel revolves around pettiness in Donostia's cultural environment, the precarious nature of work for people involved with culture, power relationships and gender treatment among them. Miren is the main character; she has agreed to be a member of a photography prize jury. She realizes that the collection of photographs that is going to win is her own work, a collection she had given to an ex-boyfriend as a present; in other words, the ex-friend uses Miren's work to win the prize. Incited by that, the main character examines her relationship with Jon and her recent past in Barcelona, and the novel becomes a tale of growing awareness. Miren then starts on a journey of escape, going to an unspecified East, to an unspecified utopian geography. The route becomes important on that journey, the metamorphosis the character undergoes along the way. Cutting her long hair herself and a relationship she has with a girl are among the most important moments in that transformation. After the transformation that takes part on the journey, during her meeting with her ex-boyfriend, he does not recognize the new Miren—short-haired, thinner, tanned, and smiling. That meeting shows that the character who has reinvented herself as a lesbian is no longer comprehensible to the eyes of a heterosexual man; she no longer answers to the criteria of comprehension for the patriarchy.

PRECARIOUS LIFE AND IMPERFECT HAPPINESS

Culture workers' precariousness is the axis to Sarriugarte's novel, but, in a wider sense, feminism has also tried to place the precariousness of life itself and men and women's vulnerability in the center of thought and political practice over recent decades, and that has left its mark in Basque novels, in novels representing LGBTQI+ lives too. Itxaro Borda's work *Ezer gabe hobe*[39] (Better without anything) provides an in-depth, wide-reaching examination of precariousness with clandestine migration from the South to the North as its subject. The text was published in 2009, in the middle of a global economic crisis, and its starting point is clandestine migration from Africa to Europe and from Mexico to the US. With one foot in the Basque Country, Borda offered a portrait of the disaster neoliberalism was causing and reflected many social conflicts and disputes.

Borda represented lives fundamentally conditioned by precariousness in her novel *Ezer gabe hobe,* and the characters' identity (and lack of identity) is another reflection of that precariousness. The writer calls the main characters Sigma and Lambda, the names of letters, making their identities vague, particularly their gender-identities. In that way Borda wrote about the precariousness which neoliberalism brings to all sides of life, as well as identity's precariousness and changeability. The thinking of Judith Butler and Monique Wittig is found throughout the novel. There are specific references to Butler's *Precarious Life*[40] throughout the text, reflections about life's "liveability," for instance. So two lines of thought put forward by Butler and feminist and queer theory come together in Borda's work: making the precariousness of life central and the need to rethink politics from that perspective, for one thing; for another, the need for gender to be seen as a performative copy of something that does not have an original. By refusing to specify the characters' genders, Borda takes their precariousness to an extreme. But, at the same time, she explores the opportunity to deconstruct identity, taking advantage of the fact that Basque has no grammatical gender. To that extent, what Borda tries to do is construct a narrative from a queer position, playing with readers' expectations. Using unmarked gender is not an objective in itself but a way of offering, rather, a deeper reflection on vulnerability and failings.

Financial precariousness brings the main characters in Ana Jaka's *Ez zen diruagatik*[41] (It wasn't for the money, 2014) together. Olga, a skeptical woman of 45, has a passive, disappointed attitude to life at the start of the novel. She has difficulty paying the rent for her flat, and so takes in a lodger called Dani, a young gay man looking for a place to live after having left his homophobic town and family and come to the city. The relationship between the two is the axis of the novel, and the connection which grows between them because of their financial needs gradually takes on other nuances. Jaka's novel, too, shows the complexity of precariousness caused by neoliberalism, and fragility is not merely financial: Olga's and Dani's lives are deeply scarred by solitude and emotional precariousness. Both characters live outside heterosexual norms: "I'll soon be fifty-five and I still don't have a job or hobbies, my own house, a family, or a little dog,"[42] Olga says to herself; Dani has broken his relationship with his family. In that fragile situation, when their two solitudes come together, financial and emotional precariousness become inseparable, and that leads to another type of caring relationship and connection.

This novel, as well as making precariousness its central theme, also explores relationships outside heterosexual norms, care networks, and the gender-roles associated with them. On the route, the characters, going from indifference about knowing each other to taking care of each other, experience a transformation in their commitments:

> "When I met Dani, before I met Mikel, for me he was just another of those fags who had a good time with other queers like himself. It's easy to accept that if you have a lot of preconceptions. It doesn't have anything to do with anybody, it doesn't affect you, to put it one way. But now I know them both, together and separately. They're flesh and blood, and they love each other. And I care about them."[43]

Crude reality is confronted, to an extent, thanks to the relationships which spring up in those fragile lives, and the novel, while avoiding a clichéd happy ending, allows a little happiness, small celebrations in life.

Telling the story of a gay couple's relationship in *Poz aldrebesa*[44] (Inside-out happiness, 2017) Juanjo Olasagarre examines the meaning of the vulnerability, caring for, and happiness of people who live outside heterosexual norms. After having a heart attack, Axi, Joseba's boyfriend, loses his memory and autonomy in daily life. Joseba begins taking care of his boyfriend, and the novel describes in detail the conflicts, difficulties, and tiredness involved in taking care of Axi. Little by little, the book describes how Joseba has to grieve for his boyfriend; he has not died, but part of him has gone for ever. But the novel's memories and grieving also take on a collective dimension, and Olasagarre draws a parallelism between memory loss and memory with regard to political violence in the Basque Country. Just as Joseba has to grieve for Axi, it is suggested that the Basque Country, as a nation, must grieve because of the armed conflict in the past if it wants to reinvent itself as a subject. A quote from Butler's *Precarious Life* opens Olasagarre's novel, where the philosopher states that accepting grief inevitably leads to a transformation of the subject, a metamorphosis that cannot be foreseen.

The novel is set in the present after ETA's final ceasefire in 2010, and it goes back to the 1990s, when Axi and Joseba met. Olasagarre gives fictional accounts of several of the debates in the Basque Country LGTB movement in those years through the characters' discussions and conversations: the relationship between national freedom and sexual freedom, the debate about proclaiming gay identity or avoiding labels, among others. Through the two characters' relationship, the writer explores the ethical revolution in the 1990s brought about by the EHGAM gay movement, appropriating Paco Vidarte's (2007) concept of *"etika marika"*[45] ("faggot ethics"). The narrative explores "faggot" ways of understanding affection and sexuality outside heterosexuality, and the opportunities for developing non-heteronormative and non-homonormative ways of living, those not based on the closed monogamous couple. However, as the novel progresses it relates several failures (the threesome which Axi and Joseba tried to form with Kenneth) which, along with Axi's hidden adultery, represent the failure of those ethics. However, that failure does not lead the character and the novel to embrace homonormativity, rather to offer a critique of gay lifestyle and several types of relationships in the neoliberal era.

Although the "faggot ethics" project is a failure to an extent and although vulnerability makes life difficult, the novel ideologically chooses joy. In line with Sara Ahmed's thesis in her essay *The Promise of Happiness*,[46] it rejects the concept of happiness, seeing the heterosexist and normative model behind it. The book concludes by proclaiming upside-down or queer joy: "I know he'll have joy later on, not happiness, but joy, in floods, on retiring, leaving the height of life uncovered like in a pool when the tide goes out. Happiness is a summer camp for heterosexuals. Only joy. Joy. Upside-down, yes, but joy."[47]

The tensions between adaptation and non-adaptation to the normative lifestyles, middle class norms and adult life demands are the keys to the novel which Kattalin Miner published the same year, *Nola heldu naiz ni honaino*[48] (How I reached here). A young girl named Jezabel is the main character. On receiving an inheritance she had not expected, a promotion, and better pay, she finds herself at the gates of the middle class. As she is about to start to comply with the conditions of "normal" adult life, she starts to have many doubts about making even the smallest decisions. Jezabel looks at the institutions, actions, and gestures of heterosexual normalcy and heteronormativity with misgiving: society based around couples, inevitable heterosexuality, going out with groups of friends … So the first-person narrator expresses her critical and sometimes ambivalent feelings about normalcy as she moves from scene to scene and reflection to reflection: "One with her child to her grandmother's town. Another to the house in Castro, and the last one to Les Landes. She was surprised the camper van and the Pyrenees hadn't been mentioned. Great, right? Yeah, and the children have a fantastic time, and the weather's good, and you can also do things without spending a lot of money."[49]

The main character becomes linked to the normality she does not want to wholly embrace. Basically, it is in the area of sexuality and desire that she finds the place to get around that, the chance to flee from normality. Breaking with her ex-girlfriend, Lucia, completely, Jezabel goes to Italy on holiday by herself. During her stay in Rome, she finds room for sexual transgression when she meets Anci and is fascinated. She agrees on sex for money with Anci, and to have specific sexual acts based on submission and dominance. So the characters' sexual encounters distance themselves from heterosexual norms in three ways: they are between women, they agree to enjoy submission and dominance, and they lead us to think about the limits of prostitution. Following the lines drawn by post-pornography and queer discourses over recent decades, then, sexuality is recognized as a possibility for transgression, as a way to create subjects outside normality. However, at the end of Miner's novel, when the character returns to her daily life, we are led to wonder whether sexual transgression is capable of changing the subject deep down, or whether norms are still deep within her, an escape from escaping.

CONCLUSIONS

I mentioned it at the start of the chapter, but perhaps it is worth saying again that I have not covered all the LGBTQI+ characters from Basque novels here, nor have I dealt with the major contributions from other genres. However, the route I suggest here may serve to draw up a sketch of certain general tendencies which future research will either take to their conclusion or turn upside down.

Literary discourse about the image of LGBTQI+ characters has ceaselessly changed over the last thirty years in continuous dialogue with many other social and cultural discourses. LGBTQI+ identities inevitably combine with other identity discourses, and, the literary field itself is constantly in contact with other social and cultural areas. There is no question that nationality is one of Basque LGBTQI+ literature's main interlocutors. As we have said, in the 1980s and 1990s, above all, the nation was a source of identity legitimization in narrative, being the all-covering umbrella that covers all other identities and struggles. National liberation, as a utopia and a revolutionary force, fundamentally conditions the novels *Haltzak badu bihotzik, Nerea eta biok,* and *Ni naizen hori,* and the tragedies portrayed in those novels are sublimed in the name of a better future. In the 2000s, novels put forward narrative strategies for lessening the weight of nationality by placing characters abroad, for instance; however, nationality was still the discourse which overshadowed LGBTQI+ identity in many of these stories. On the other hand, in novels in the 2010s the national discourse became less important, and it is not represented as a conflict in most works by the new generation of writers. However, the national conflict is still to be found in the work of novelists born in the 1960s (Olasagarre, Borda), but now as a memory issue, something from the past, and not as a source of tension which conditions LGBTQI+ people's identities and lives.

National discourses also permeate gender discourses in these novels. The national struggle and the armed struggle connected with it reproduce the masculine and feminine roles: a militarized masculinity for men (military service, the armed struggle) and, for women, femininity linked with care (soldiers' mothers and carers). In some novels the prevalence of those traditional roles in opposition to people's will and desires gets in the way of the possibility of escaping from heterosexual norms; in later novels, the characters who confront those traditional roles proclaim themselves to be gays or lesbians.

There is also a difference connected with gender when we compare Basque narratives depicting gay and lesbian lives. In narratives about gay characters, homosexuality is a truth they discover, something they verify and from which there is no going back, something unconnected to individuals' will and which often brings a tragic destiny with it. On the other hand, lesbianism is seen as an option, a chance for the subject to reinvent herself and escape from the heterosexual regime. There is also greater flexibility and ambiguity in narrative terms too when lesbian characters and relationships are put into fiction: in some cases the boundaries between friendship and erotic relationships are not clear; in other cases the frontier between reality and fantasy is more blurred, and characters can often be seen as projections. Perhaps influenced by that plasticity of identity, in Borda's novels there is a desire to reshape national identity from a lesbian perspective; in Olasagarre's novels, on the other hand, there is conflict and competition between the two identities rather than a proposal to form a hybrid identity.

At the same time, LGBTQI+ characters in Basque novels take different positions with regard to identity. In 2004's *Ezinezko maletak,* the character Bazter proclaims himself to be gay, and Amaia Ezpeldoi appears as a lesbian in 2007; however, in previous novels gays, lesbians, and trans characters do not proclaim their identity. In these Basque novels, characters are conflicted when it comes to declaring themselves to be gay or lesbian, but that is also a strategy for confronting other types of social norms and to be able to lead livelier existences. In novels in which there is no LGBTQI+ identity or collective identification, characters who desire members of the same sex face tragic destinies, and they are often condemned to solitude.

These literary discourses are also connected with known literary traditions. It is significant that the main characters in three of the novels from the 1990s which I have examined are closely connected with the literary world: two of them teach literature (*Nerea eta biok, Haltzak badu bihotzik*), and a third is a bookseller (*Ni naizen hori*). All three of them have writers who had non-heterosexual normative relationships or who had written about LGBTQI+ subjects as their figures of reference (Sade, Genet, Gide, Woolf, Colette . . .), and in some cases the novels deal with the tradition of narrative about admiration for lives on the margin. It may be seen that in these initiation novels references and inspiration have come from the tendencies of a literary tradition rather than from personal or collective experiences. In more recent novels, however, literary references have been used to create the authors' own images.

On the other hand, over the last ten years queer and feminist theory has become the main source of reference in many novels rather than literary tradition. Butler's, Wittig's, and Ahmed's works are sometimes implicitly present, other times explicitly so, in novels from the last decade. The most recent narrative explores subjects including the precariousness of life, the performative side of identity, and critiques of happiness and normativity. This meeting point between literary and philosophical discourse also influences the novels' structuring and narrative, making them hybrids to make space for ideas, and also making use of experimentation with form (by removing gender markings, for instance). In the same way, we can conclude from this short description that it is impossible to understand the transformation of the representation of LGBTQI+ characters as a lineal advance which leads to a final normalization. To that extent, it should be emphasized that tension with regard to homonormativity has been one of the major issues in novels from recent years. The interpretations suggested here also state that these tensions about homonormativity are mostly negotiated within the context of couples' relationships.

I questioned the term "LGBTQI+ Literature" at the start of this chapter. After reviewing this literature, I do not believe that in Basque literature it had the same meaning in the 1980s as it has in the 2010s. In the early years it is mostly heterosexual writers' representations of LGBTQI+ characters that we have to take into consideration; later on, in the 2000s, gay and lesbian writers began to appear, and networks and complicity have grown between them. From the perspective of literary criticism, on the other hand, work has been done to read these narratives in the LGBTQI+ context (and not with a supposedly neutral literary and linguistic criteria) above from the 2000s onward, although queer criticism remains a weak field of study in Basque culture.

LGBTQI+ characters have gone from being represented in the literary field to being the subject of representations, and we have started to interpret depending on the tools available to us. Writing about ourselves and developing our own keys for interpretation have also influenced the image of LGBTQI+ life: several characteristics that describe the novels published in the 1990s (a tendency to alarmism and tragedy, LGBTQI+ characters' isolation and solitude . . .) no longer define current novel writing. However, I would say that in the jump from being represented as objects to being shown as subjects, nuances have become more important and strategies have been developed to make LGBTQI+ characters survive. Non-heteronormative people depicted in recent novels are able to find the way to be happy or experience joy at times, and, it seems to me, that Basque LGBTQI+ readers' reality and the fictions created by Basque literature have become closer to each other. In fact, this literature which goes beyond clichés and represents Basque LGBTQI+ characters in fiction does not only present us with a specific reality, it also finds the universal within the specific.

BIBLIOGRAPHY

Ahmed, Sara. *The promise of happiness*. Durham, NC, and London: Duke University Press, 2010.

Apalategi, Ur. "Errealismoaren eraberritzea eta kokapena 90eko hamarkadako euskal literaturan," in *Azken aldiko euskal narratiba. Sortzaileak eta irakurleak*, edited by Kirmen Uribe Urbieta, 41-56. Bilbao: Udako Euskal Unibertsitatea, 200.

Apaolaza, Uxue. *Mea culpa*. Donostia: Elkar, 2011.

Arana, Aitor. *Aita-semeak*. Donostia: Hiria, 1995.

———. *Onan*. Tafalla: Txalaparta, 2000.

Arregi Diaz de Heredia, Rikardo. "Aspaldiko hitzaldi bat gogoan" in *Desira desordenatuak*, edited by Ibon Egaña, 43-58. Donostia: Utriusque Vasconiae, 2010.

Ayerbe, Mikel. "Ustekabeak, ezusteak eta esanezinak: ezkututik agerira?" in *Desira desordenatuak*, edited by Ibon Egaña, 59-86. Donostia: Utriusque Vasconiae, 2010.

Borda, Itxaro, *Bizi nizano munduan*. Zarautz: Susa, 1996.

———. "Klara eta biok," Maiatz 16 (1985): 15-23.

———. *Amorezko pena baño*. Zarautz: Susa, 1996.

———. *Bakean ützi arte*. Zarautz: Susa, 1994.

———. *Boga boga*. Zarautz: Susa, 2012.

———. *Ezer gabe hobe*. Zarautz: Susa, 2009.

———. *Jalgi hadi plazara*. Zarautz: Susa, 2007.

Butler, Judith. *Precarious life*. London and New York: Verso, 2004.

Castillo Etxano, Isa and Iratxe Retolaza, eds. *Genero ariketak: feminismoaren subjektuak*. Donostia: edo!, 2013.

Egaña, Ibon, ed. *Desira desordenatuak: queer irakurketak (euskal) literaturaz* (Donostia: Utriusque Vasconiae, 2010.

Gabilondo, Joseba. "Itxaro Borda: melancholic migrancy and the writing of a national lesbian self." Anuario del Seminario de Filología Vasca Julio de Urquijo: *International Journal of Basque Linguistics and Philology* 34, num. 2 (2000): 291-314

Gabiria, Julen. *Connemara gure bihotzetan*. Donostia: Elkar, 2000.

González, Helena. *Elas e o paraguas totalizador*. Vigo: Edicións Xerais, 2005.

Gorrindo, Karlos. *Ni naizen hori*. Tafalla: Txalaparta, 1994.

Jaka, Ana. *Ez zen diruagatik*. Donostia: Elkar, 2014.

Jimenez, Irati. *Bat, bi, Manchester*. Donostia: Elkar, 2006.

Lamarca, Iñigo. *Gay nauzu*. Irun: Alberdania, 1999.

Mendiguren, Iñaki. *Haltzak badu bihotzik*. Donostia: Elkar, 1990.

Miner, Kattalin. *Nola heldu naiz ni honaino*. Donostia: Elkar, 2017.

Mintegi, Laura. *Nerea eta biok*. Tafalla: Txalaparta, 1994.

Olasagarre, Juanjo. *Ezinezko maletak*. Zarautz: Susa, 2004.

———. *Poz aldrebesa*. Zarautz: Susa, 2017.

Retolaza, Iratxe. "Amaia Ezpeldoi detektibea: kode-urratzailea eta ibiltari sinbolikoa.". In *% 100 Basque*. Forum Hitzaldiak. Edited by Bilbo Zaharra Euskaltegia, 53-64. Bilbao: Bilbo Zaharra Euskaltegia.

Sarriugarte, Danele. *Azala erre*. Donostia: Elkar, 2018.

Vidarte, Paco. *Ética marica*. Madrid: Egales, 2007.

Yuval-Davies, Nira. *Gender and Nation*. London: Sage Publications, 1997.

NOTES

1   This chapter is part of the research project "Gender identities and transmision of socio-political discourses in Basque literature (US 18/39)," funded by UPV/EHU.

2   Joseba Gabilondo. "Itxaro Borda: melancholic migrancy and the writing of a national lesbian self." *Anuario del Seminario de Filología Vasca Julio de Urquijo: International Journal of Basque Linguistics and Philology 34, num. 2* (2000): 291-314

3   Ibon Egaña (ed.) *Desira desordenatuak: queer irakurketak (euskal) literaturaz* (Donostia: Utriusque Vasconiae, 2010).

4   Isa Castillo Etxano and Iratxe Retolaza (ed.) *Genero ariketak: feminismoaren subjektuak.* (Donostia: edo!, 2013).

5   Several events about the image of gays and lesbians in Basque literature were held in the 2000s: In June 2011 Gasteiz's Lesgaytegia organized a roundtable discussion in which Andolin Eguzkitza, Rikardo Arregi Diaz de Heredia, and Juanjo Olasagarre took part. In 2006 Itxaro Borda and Mikel Ayerbe each gave talks as part of a course organized by the Basque Summer University, talking, respectively, from the creator's and the critic's point of view. In 2007 another round table discussion was held in Donostia, organized by EHGAM, and there, along with Arregi and Olasagarre, Angel Erro, Aitor Arana and Itxaro Borda took part.

6   Itxaro Borda, "Klara eta biok," Maiatz 16 (1985), 15-23

7   Iñaki Mendiguren, *Haltzak badu bihotzik* (Donostia: Elkar, 1990).

8   Laura Mintegi, *Nerea eta biok* (Tafalla: Txalaparta, 1994)

9   Ibid., 36

10   Ibid., 33.

11   Ibid., 44.

12 Ibid., 31.

13 Nira Yuval-Davies, *Gender and Nation* (London: Sage Publications).

14 Karlos Gorrindo, *Ni naizen hori* (Tafalla: Txalaparta, 1994).

15 Ibid, 33.

16 Ibid, 127.

17 González, *Elas e o paraguas totalizador.*

18 Ur Apalategi, "Errealismoaren eraberritzea eta kokapena 90eko hamarkadako euskal literaturan," in *Azken aldiko euskal narratiba. Sortzaileak eta irakurleak*, ed. Kirmen Uribe Urbieta (Bilbao: Udako Euskal Unibertsitatea, 2001), 41-56.

19 Arana. *Aita-semeak* (Donostia: Hiria, 1995); Arana. *Onan* (Tafalla: Txalaparta, 2000)

20 Iñigo Lamarca, *Gay nauzu* (Irun: Alberdania, 1999).

21 Rikardo Arregi Diaz de Heredia, "Aspaldiko hitzaldi bat gogoan" in *Desira desordenatuak*, 43-58.

22 Ayerbe. "Ustekabeak, ezusteak eta esanezinak: ezkututik agerira?" 59-86.

23 Gabiria. *Connemara gure bihotzetan* (Donostia: Elkar, 2000).

24 Olasagarre. *Ezinezko maletak* (Zarautz: Susa, 2004).

25 Jimenez. *Bat, bi, Manchester* (Donostia: Elkar, 2006).

26 Ibid.

27 Borda. *Bakean ützi arte* (Zarautz: Susa, 1994).

28 Borda. *Amorezko pena baño* (Zarautz: Susa, 1996).

29 Borda, *Bizi nizano munduan* (Zarautz: Susa, 1996).

30 Retolaza. "Amaia Ezpeldoi detektibea: kode-urratzailea eta ibiltari sinbolikoa," 53-64.

31 Gabilondo. "Itxaro Borda: melancholic migrancy and the writing of a national lesbian self"

32 Borda, *Jalgi hadi plazara* (Zarautz: Susa, 2007).

33 Ibid., 152.

34 Ibid., 23.

35 Ibid., 218.

36 Borda. *Boga boga* (Zarautz: Susa, 2012).

37 Apaolaza. *Mea culpa* (Donostia: Elkar, 2011).

38 Sarriugarte. *Azala erre* (Donostia: Elkar, 2018).

39 Borda. *Ezer gabe hobe* (Zarautz: Susa, 2009).

40 Butler. *Precarious life* (London/New York: Verso, 2004).

41 Jaka. *Ez zen diruagatik* (Donostia: Elkar, 2014).

42 Ibid., 13.

43 Ibid., 113.

44 Olasagarre. *Poz aldrebesa* (Zarautz: Susa, 2017).

45 Vidarte. *Ética marica* (Madrid: Egales, 2007).

46 Ahmed. *The Promise of Happiness* (Durham, NC: Duke University Press, 2010) .

47 Olasagarre, *Poz aldrebesa*, 416.

48 Miner, *Nola heldu naiz ni honaino* (Donostia: Elkar, 2017).

49 Ibid., 54.

Index

X
Xut, 145

Y
Yemen, 13, 18
#YoTeCreo, 99

Z
Zacharias Wilsma, 2
Zanardelli Code, 4, 20
Zanardelli, Giuseppe, 4
zoophilia, 2

About the Authors

ANDREA BERTOMEU NAVARRO, BA and MA in Advanced Studies in Law at the University of Alicante, is University Specialist in political integration and economic union in the EU. She got her PhD at the University of the Basque Country. She has been professor of Public International Law and International Relations at the University of Alicante (2011-2014), as well as Academic Secretary of the Interuniversity Center for European Studies of the University of Alicante and Coordinator of various Jean Monnet projects on European integration. Her lines of research focus on the respect for fundamental rights as a limit to EU asylum and immigration policies, with special attention to the principle of non-refoulement.

JOKIN AZPIAZU CARBALLO, BA in sociology and MA in Feminist and Gender Studies from the University of the Basque Country. He currently works on the European project Universities Supporting Victims of Sexual Violence (USVSV) and is a professor in the Department of Sociology of the University of the Basque Country. His work as a researcher has been focused in recent years on the study of power relations from an intersectional feminist perspective. He has participated in the European project GAP Work against gender-related violence (DAPHNE) and is currently a researcher in the mentioned USVSV project. He participates in the SIMReF-JovenTIC research group, and in the SIMReF collective since 2011. He has published several articles in academic journals, as well as the book *Masculinities and feminism* (Editorial Virus, 2017) that gathers the reflections of that research and collective reflections after it.

MARÍA RUIZ TORRADO is a professor in the Department of Philosophy and Social Anthropology at the University of the Basque Country (UPV/EHU). After studying history (EHU, 2006) as well as social and cultural anthropology (EHU, 2008), she earned a Master's degree in Feminist and Gender Studies at EHU in 2010. The topic of her PhD dissertation at EHU was "Jail as a gender institution: gender discrimination, resistance practices and agency among women imprisoned in the Basque Country" (2016). She is a member of the AFIT Feminist Anthropology Research Group at EHU and has published several book chapters and articles in specialized journals, among them, "Sexual-affective resistance in prison: an approach to the agency of incarcerated women" (Mari Luz Esteban and Jone M. Hernández García (coord.), *Feminist ethnographies. A look at the 21st century from the Basque anthropology*, (Edicions Bellaterra.) Barcelona, 2018, pp. 159-181) and *Kartzela genero-erakunde bezala: bereizkeriak, erresistentziak eta agentzia Euskal Herrian espetxeratutako emakumeen artean* [*Prison as a gender institution: discrimination, resistance and agency among women imprisoned in the Basque Country*] (UEU, Bilbao, 2017).

ABEL DÍAZ, M.A in History from the University of La Laguna ULL (Tenerife), he has completed the Interuniversity Master's Degree in Contemporary History at the University of the Basque Country (EHU), where he is currently working on his doctoral thesis within the Contemporary History Program, in the field of homosexuality and normative masculinity during the Francoist dictatorship (1939-1976). In 2015 he obtained a predoctoral contract as a researcher in training (PIF) at the University of the Basque Country. The objective of his doctoral research project is to analyze the historical construction of homosexual identity throughout the Franco dictatorship, from a non-essentialist perspective, through the analysis of the social meanings that homosexuality acquires in each moment and in each speech.

IBON EGAÑA holds a PhD in Comparative Literature and Literary Studies from the University of the Basque Country. Since 2006 he is a professor in the Department of Didactics of Language and Literature at the Faculty of Education, Anthropology and Philosophy on the campus of Donostia. His research works focus on contemporary Basque literature from perspectives such as the sociology of literature or queer theories. Currently, his research is focused on the representation of political violence in Basque literature from a gender perspective. He has published numerous articles in scientific journals and he is the coordinator of several books, among them, *Maldetan Sagarrak* (UEU, 2006) a collection of readings on the literary representation of political violence and, *Desira desordenatuak* (Utriusque Vasconiae, 2010) a compilation of Queer criticism about Basque literature). More recently he has published *Izan gabe denaz* (Utriusque Vasconiae, 2015), a sociological approach to journalistic criticism in Basque between 1975 and 2005.

XABIER IRUJO is the director of the Center for Basque Studies at the University of Nevada, Reno, where he is professor of Basque studies. He was the first guest research scholar of the Manuel Irujo Chair at the University of Liverpool and has taught seminars on genocide and cultural genocide at Boise State University and at the University of California, Santa Barbara. He holds three Master's degrees in linguistics, history and philosophy and has two PhDs in history and philosophy. Dr. Irujo has lectured in various American and European universities and published on issues related to Basque history and politics, and has specialized along his career in genocide studies, researching periods of Basque history related to both physical and cultural extermination. Dr. Irujo has authored more than fifteen books and a number of articles in specialized journals and has received awards and distinctions at national and international level. His recent books include *Gernika 1937: The Market Day Massacre* (University of Nevada Press, 2015) and *Gernika: Genealogy of a Lie* (Sussex Academic Press, 2018).

MARÍA GÓMEZ holds an international Master's in Peace Studies from the Jaume I University of Castelló (2016). In 2018, she completed the Master's Degree in Feminist and Gender Studies at the University of the Basque Country. Journalist and writer, she is currently developing her dissertation at the Program in Feminist Studies of the University of the Basque Country. Her object of study has been intersexualities. She has participated, since 2017, in the Bottom Up project of Comprehensive Care for Minors –Intersex– with Different Sexual Development at the Pediatric Surgery Service of the Donostia Hospital in Gipuzkoa (Basque Country). She collaborates with the Basque Feminist Magazine Pikara, and is the author of several articles, including "I am Lola and I am Intersexual" and "The I has started to come out of the closet." She has highlighted both in the field of research and activism, and her field of study is intersexualities, intersectional feminist perspectives, queer theory and the human rights of intersex people.

MARTA LUXÁN BA in sociology at the University of the Basque Country (1992) and PhD in demography at the Universidad Autónoma de Barcelona (2000). She is an associate professor at the University of the Basque Country and responsible for the Master's on Feminist and Gender Studies. Her research covers three main areas of interest: demography, research methodology and feminist methodology and social movements. She is a member of the Feminist Anthropology research Group (AFIT) and of the Interdisciplinary Seminar of Feminist Methodology (SIMReF). She has been the principal local researcher of the European Project "Universities Supporting Victims of Sexual Violence (USVSV)" and is working on the project "Nuevas solidaridades, reciprocidades y alianzas: la emergencia de espacios colaborativos de participación política y redefinición de la ciudadanía". She has also published several book chapters and articles in specialized journals.

JONE M. HERNÁNDEZ, MA in Information Sciences and Social and Political Sciences from the University of the Basque Country (EHU) and PhD in Social Anthropology from the same university. She is currently a professor of Social Anthropology at EHU both in undergraduate and postgraduate levels and she is part of the research group of Feminist Anthropology AFIT. For two decades she has been investigating issues related to the language (Basque) and Basque culture, youth, leisure time and sports from a feminist and gender point of view. She is the author of numerous publications, the last of which are related to bertsolaritza or Basque improvisational poetry, among them, Etnografías feministas. Una mirada al siglo XXI desde la antropología vasca (Edicions Bellaterra, 2018) and "Algunas instrucciones para abrir la caja negra del conocimiento feminista" (Disparidades. Revista de Antropología, vol. 74, No. 1, 2019).

MAIALEN ARANGUREN, MA in History from the University of the Basque Country. She is member of the Experiencia Moderna Research Group (UPV/EHU) and she is completing her PhD dissertation under the directorship of Drs. Mercedes Arbaiza and Nerea Aresti on "The political anatomy of the feminist body. The autonomous movement of Basque women (1975-1994)". It focuses on the shaping and consolidation of the feminist movement in the Basque Country after the end of the dictatorship in 1975. From the perspective of gender discourses, her aim is to study the conditions that paved the way to the creation of a new political subject in the Basque Country: the feminists. She was a visiting graduate student at the University of California, San Diego (UCSD), under the supervision of historian Pamela Radcliff. With Nerea Aresti, she has co-authored the book chapter "Women Above All: The Autonomous Basque Feminist Movement (1973-1994)", in Bermúdez and Johnson, *A New History of Iberian Feminism*, 2018.

Made in the USA
Monee, IL
23 November 2021